Pull

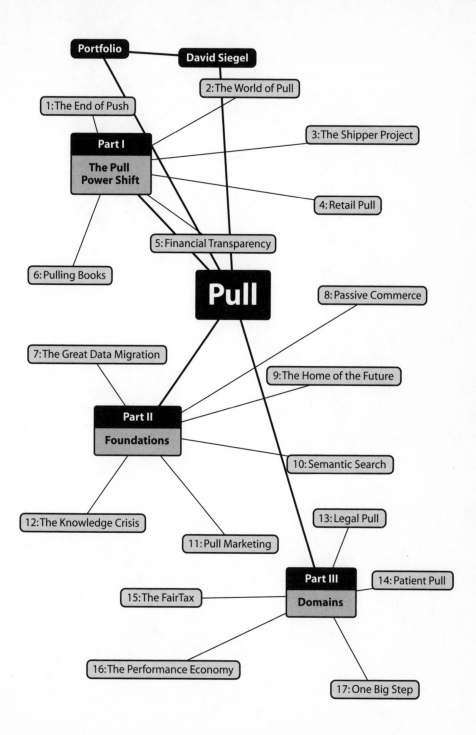

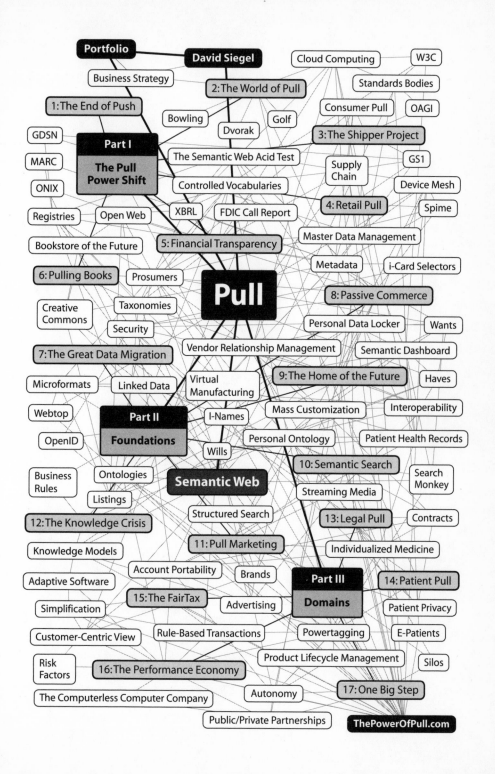

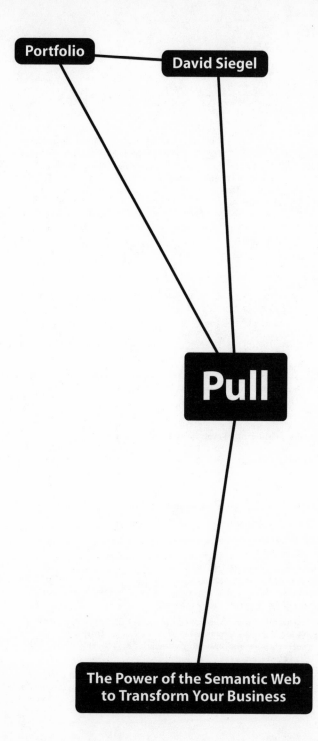

Portfolio

David Siegel

Pull

The Power of the Semantic Web
to Transform Your Business

PORTFOLIO
Published by the Penguin Group
Penguin Group (USA) Inc., 375 Hudson Street, New York, New York 10014, U.S.A. • Penguin Group
(Canada), 90 Eglinton Avenue East, Suite 700, Toronto, Ontario, Canada M4P 2Y3 • (a division of
Pearson Penguin Canada Inc.) • Penguin Books Ltd, 80 Strand, London WC2R 0RL, England • Pen-
guin Ireland, 25 St. Stephen's Green, Dublin 2, Ireland (a division of Penguin Books Ltd) • Penguin
Books Australia Ltd, 250 Camberwell Road, Camberwell, Victoria 3124, Australia (a division of Pearson
Australia Group Pty Ltd) • Penguin Books India Pvt Ltd, 11 Community Centre, Panchsheel Park,
New Delhi - 110 017, India • Penguin Group (NZ), 67 Apollo Drive, Rosedale, North Shore 0632, New
Zealand (a division of Pearson New Zealand Ltd) • Penguin Books (South Africa) (Pty) Ltd, 24 Sturdee
Avenue, Rosebank, Johannesburg 2196, South Africa

Penguin Books Ltd, Registered Offices:
80 Strand, London WC2R 0RL, England

First published in 2009 by Portfolio,
a member of Penguin Group (USA) Inc.

10 9 8 7 6 5 4 3 2 1

LIBRARY OF CONGRESS CATALOGING IN PUBLICATION DATA

Siegel, David.
Pull : the power of the semantic web to transform your business / David Siegel.
    p. cm.
Includes bibliographical references and index.
ISBN 978-1-59184-277-4
1. Electronic commerce. 2. Semantic Web. 3. Information technology—Management. 4. Internet
marketing. I. Title.
HF5548.32.S5525 2009
658.8'072—dc22   2009035779

Printed in the United States of America
Set in Adobe Garamond Pro with Myriad Pro

To the thousands of people helping make this dream a reality

Contents

Part III: Domains

Introduction

THINK OF EVERY FORM YOU HAVE EVER FILLED OUT and every form that has your name on it. You've probably filled out more forms, both on paper and online, than you would like to see all together in the same room. So imagine that you can see all the documents in all the filing cabinets and all the databases, all across the globe: medical charts, prescriptions, tests, credit statements, receipts, school registrations, government forms, packages, memos, emails, hotel registrations, badges, tickets, contracts, subscriptions, and little scraps of data drifting down the electronic highway. Looking down from above, you might not be surprised to see that your information has really spread.

Put a small dot on the map for every piece of your information – the map will be covered with thousands of small dots. Back up further and you will see plenty of dots on cities in Utah, Florida, California, Delaware, and South Dakota, as well as the Philippines, India, Singapore, South Africa, Belgium, England, France, Canada, Iceland, and Mexico, even though you may never have been to any of these places. Now look online – you will find your information in far-flung databases, web sites you've never visited, companies you've never heard of, even hacker hideouts.

That interactive map of your information exhaust is the first "slide"

I'll show as we take a journey through the changing world of information. Today, the information ecosystem is a loosely connected, ad hoc collage of data that generally doesn't work very hard. It is complete with partners, predators, and parasites. For our companies and our personal lives, information is out of control. It's time we did something about it. This book is that something.

> **Warning: Business Acceleration Ahead!**

This book describes **the pull era**, where customers pull everything to them on demand – products, services, information, knowledge, and advice. Much of the foundation for pulling is called the **semantic web**, a new way of packaging information to make it much more useful and reusable. Over the next ten to twenty years, it will change business from a lead-push model to a pull-follow model of interacting with customers.

Together, we'll fly low over the semantic web infrastructure as it's being built today. We'll see how different things will be in just a few short years. Much of the discussion will be technical, so be prepared for new terms and concepts, and some new jargon (though I'll try to keep it to a minimum). Watch for the words "quadrillion" and "quintillion." When you say to yourself, That can't possibly happen, ask what you would have predicted back in 1990, before the World Wide Web changed the business landscape forever. Rather than looking for proven strategies, I ask you to consider the possibilities. As you learn about new game-changing technologies, keep looking for the management mind shift you'll need to go bravely into the world of pull.

In **Part I**, I'll give the basic definitions and principles of pulling information. Then I'll show three industries already ahead of the curve, learning their way from push to pull. **Part II** describes most of the principles and mechanisms that will change the way information will be used in the next five to ten years, both by consumers, who will lead with their demands, and by businesses, who will have to respond.

Part III looks at how industries will change when we start pulling information. We will improve the legal profession, get health care working for patients, and, just for fun, blow up the income tax. The coming performance economy from this completely new perspective. Finally, I'll talk about how you can get your company started and build your own road map from push to pull.

There are barriers and risks to adopting these principles, yet I argue that the risks of not doing so are even higher. While early adopters will pick the low-hanging fruit, companies that wait behind their legacy business processes will find much of their lunch eaten in the early years.

This book is guaranteed to raise more questions than it answers. After reading it, come to **ThePowerofPull.com** to learn more, see what people are saying, and join the conversation. You'll see a lot of web sites mentioned in this book. There's no need to type them into your browser – you can follow along using the links for each chapter on the site for the book.

Boldface type indicates structural markers in the text, to provide signposts as you read or go back to review previously read chapters.

Note: Macroeconomic factors can crack any crystal ball. Any dates mentioned are purely to give an idea of the range, not to be specific deadlines.

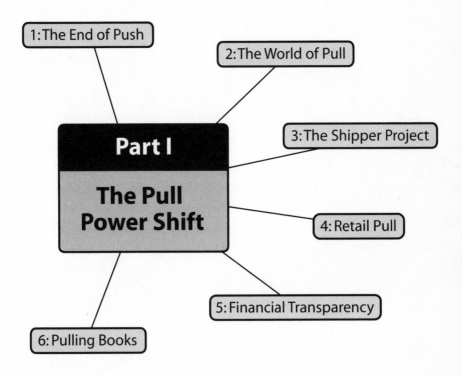

1: The End of Push

2: The World of Pull

3: The Shipper Project

Part I

The Pull Power Shift

4: Retail Pull

5: Financial Transparency

6: Pulling Books

1: The End of Push

Pull Concept: Incremental Improvements Won't Work

> *In a time of drastic change, it is the LEARNERS who inherit the future. The LEARNED usually find themselves equipped to live in a world that no longer exists.*
>
> – Eric Hoffer

HERE'S THE REAL PROBLEM IN A NUTSHELL: what we're doing in business isn't working. We're barely hanging on. And we're either frustrated or in denial about it. If you extrapolate from the way we were doing business ten years ago, through where we are today, to where business will be in ten years, we can't get there by doing more of the same thing. The way we solve problems today won't scale up to meet the ever-increasing demands of our customers.

First, let's look at the problem from a few angles. Rather than cite research, I'm going to paraphrase what I've heard people say in meetings, in articles, and online.

The CTO: "We're still spending 75 percent of our IT budget maintaining our existing systems. I've gotten it down from 80 percent a year ago, but how can we try something new if I have to spend most of my budget keeping things from breaking? Our vendors have us locked in on life support – for *them*!"

The VP, Distribution: "I just got back from a supply chain meeting in Europe. They are light-years ahead of us. The way they use information makes their stores ten times more productive than ours. I figure we lose 12 percent of sales simply because the product isn't on the shelf or available when a customer asks for it."

The VP, Marketing: "We're losing market share. We're not the authoritative source we were five years ago. Twenty-five percent of our customers do product research from their mobile phones while shopping in the store! They're even reading the bar codes themselves! There are 30 billion web pages, and we're on about a dozen of them. Our site is rated number seven by comScore in the key searches we monitor. Might as well be twenty-seven!"

The Research Manager: "Productivity. Most of my researchers spend their time looking for stuff. We measured it – 57 percent for the average researcher. One of my consultants calculated that we spend $550 to create an average document here, and we're surrounded by documents![1] Our average researcher gets 160 emails a day. If even half of those are meaningful, you have to send 80 responses a day just to keep from falling behind. And these are the people we're counting on for our next generation of products."

The Hiring Manager: "On an average day, this company loses 37 people and hires 55. Do you know how many people it takes me to do that? We're losing the know-how people build over many years working here, and we probably miss 20 percent of the best candidates because they take jobs before we can get to them."

The Product Manager: "The real problem is brand erosion. The quality of our products is as high as ever, but customers don't see the value we add. The market is starting to splinter in ways we can't even track, and customers don't see our brand as a central part of their lives."

The COO: "We've gotten too damn good at doing what we did a few years ago. Our processes are optimized for markets that no longer exist. Change management is just a buzzword; people don't take it seriously. Skill sets aren't really changing fast enough to meet today's challenges, let alone tomorrow's. We're driving a cruise ship in a white-water environment."

The CIO: "I'm looking at the big picture. The worldwide economy is a bigger factor than any of these things. Humans now generate more than 200 *exabytes* of information per year. That's the equivalent of twenty *million* Libraries of Congress. Two years ago, it was all about prosperity. Now, it's uncertainty. Price of oil and exchange rates now have as big an impact as market forecasts. Everything is much harder to predict. The big problem is volatility, and it's here to stay."

The Executive Vice President: "We have great managers. We can execute on anything. What we don't have is leaders. We're losing ground because we're not inspiring our people or our customers, period."

The Venture Capitalist: "I've got a handful of small companies in the transitional space between Web 2.0 and the semantic web. What I want to know is this: when should I start investing in fully semantic solutions? It seems it's always on the horizon but it never arrives."

The Entrepreneur: "The web is broken. We are all using twenty different web sites to do twenty different things. We spend our days going here and there, logging in, giving our credentials and credit card numbers, searching over and over trying to find what we are looking for. I want to build a site to solve a particular problem, but my customers don't need another web site. They need fewer web sites and more functionality!"

What is *your* biggest issue? What is holding your company back from continued growth and profitability? I want you to carry that issue with you on our journey and see whether I address it. Our goal is not to make incremental improvements but to find a new learning curve, following our customers into a radically different future, reshaping our companies as we change from pushing information to pulling it.

2: The World of Pull

Pull Concept: Generating Metadata Automatically

> *We need languages for expressing the relationships between different sorts of data: a "semantic web" which will let all the data be seen as one big database. The semantic web will be revolutionary for e-commerce.*
>
> – Tim Berners-Lee

THIS IS THE STORY OF PULLING INFORMATION – getting what we need, when we need it. It started in about 1980 and should be mostly complete by about 2030. We're about 1 percent of the way through this transition, the first new way to use information in 4,000 years. It has profound implications for how we perceive and manage our businesses.

Using a few examples, I want to show how different things will be when we start pulling. Then I will give a few definitions of terms we'll need as we go into the chapters that follow.

The Grocery Store Question

Let's start with a quiz. Suppose you run a large grocery store with many cash registers. Four of the registers are dedicated to shoppers with ten items or fewer, which encourages people to come in and make a small purchase when they might not otherwise because the lines are too long. You hire a consultant to help you look at your business, and she says, "You're penalizing your best customers. It's fine to open checkout lanes for people with only a few items, but you don't make much money off them, and they could be just as happy getting a few things from the store down the street. What happens if someone has two carts full of groceries? Shouldn't she go to the front of the line? Shouldn't she be treated like gold? I think you should dedicate three cashiers to ten items or fewer and one cashier solely to people with two carts or more."

Now, here's the question: do you take the consultant's advice? Are you ready to compare your answer with mine?

My answer is *that if one single customer waits in line for a cashier, that's one too many.* Your consultant is thinking about making an old system marginally better, a little more customer-centered, while new technologies will wipe out cashiers altogether, saving you money and giving your customers the service they deserve.

How, then, will your customers get out of the store without becoming cashiers themselves? The answer to that question is in Chapter 4. Now let's look at an industry where the power shift has already taken place.

Bowling

By the end of the nineteenth century, bowling as we know it was played in many states on the East Coast of the United States. Back then, each bowling center had its own rules, balls, lanes, and pins. Pinsetters picked up the pins by hand and placed them – more or less – back where they were supposed to be after each roll. In 1895, Joe Thum and a group of bowlers from various states founded the American Bowling Congress and standardized the game. By 1914, when Brunswick introduced an 8½-inch rubber ball to replace the old wooden balls, most bowling centers complied with the new standards, the playing field leveled, and tournaments became popular. Because of the standards, some 70 million people in the United States bowl each year.[2]

In 1952, the first AMC pin-setting machines rolled off the production lines and quickly replaced the hired help, improving pin placement and reducing costs. But, from an information standpoint, bowling was still in the Dark Ages.

When I started bowling in the late 1960s, my friends and I registered at the front desk, got our shoes and balls, and asked who is keeping score. Everyone would look at me, so I received a big piece of paper and a pencil with an eraser. I wrote down all the names and called them out as their turn came up. As each person bowled, I made pencil marks on the paper and added up the score, according to the sometimes tricky bowling math. Occasionally, I made mistakes and had to redo the calculations. In the end, I produced a big sheet of paper with many marks on it, and that was our score.

The power shift took place in the mid-1980s as bowling facilities switched to pin-setting machines that report the score to a computer, which automatically displays the score after each person bowls. No longer do you have to worry about scoring – you just type in the names of the bowlers and start. To generate the score, you just roll the ball down the lane. This innovation (along with loud music and purple lights) is responsible for the rejuvenation of the sport. And yet, we still have to enter our names into that computer before we can start bowling.

The final phase of the transformation will take place when you simply walk into any bowling alley, grab a pair of shoes from the wall, find an unused lane, and start bowling. When you're done, the bowling alley will automatically charge your account for every frame, then add your score to your personal online data locker (Chapter 8), where all your bowling statistics live in one place. No matter where you bowl, every frame is recorded in your online data locker, where you can chart your progress and use online tools to help manage your bowling life. Because of the worldwide metadata standards, you'll enter a tournament against thousands of other bowlers in hundreds of cities around the globe on the same day – the software compares your scores and declares the winners.

That's pulling information. Bowling has made the critical transition from the customer telling the system what the score is *to the system telling the customer what the score is*. While other industries are still stuck in nineteenth-century information models, the bowling industry is one of the very few that have already gone through this important inflection (turning) point. It's an incremental step to add the rest of the building blocks that will serve bowling for the rest of the century.

Golf

Now let's look at golf. We want to make golf less frustrating, not by making faster carts or increasing the diameter of the cup but by reversing the scoring mechanism. It will take years for this to develop, but eventually the clubs, balls, and cups will all communicate with each other and transmit information to your personal golf data locker, where your score shows up instantly. You can see it on the electronic scorecard that looks remarkably like your phone. In fact, it *is* your phone. You don't tell the display what your score is – the display tells you. You don't count your strokes – your phone can tell you how many strokes you've taken and how far your ball is from the hole. Your phone can tell you which club is missing from your bag and show its location on a map. Your phone alerts you to weather changes or important messages, and it can find your ball in the tall grass. You can see each stroke on a map of the course, and you can compare shots on the same hole from previous games or with other players. Others watching remotely can see your statistics in real time if you want them to.

From an information standpoint, bowling is at the front of the curve; golf is at the back. We are still pushing information in golf, as we are in almost every other area of our lives. This is one of the few industries where the technology to improve the flow of information still hasn't really been invented yet. We are still using little wooden pencils on paper scorecards. It will take at least ten years before golf reaches its inflection point. It will take that long for many industries, and each will have its own blurry inflection point.

Facebook

The other day, I called my father's home. My stepmother answered, and we talked for a while. Then she passed the phone to my dad, who said, "Did you wish your stepmother a happy birthday?" My bad! I had completely forgotten her birthday, talked to her, and didn't say anything. She certainly got that message!

I thought, that's not fair! If you're my friend or relative and it's your birthday today, I count on my Facebook page to tell me that. If you're on my friend list, Facebook will tell me it's your birthday. Why should I have to maintain a list of birthdays and anniversaries? Why don't you just connect to me on Facebook, so the relationships online mirror the relationships offline? If I take you off my friend list, I'll no longer learn about your birthday in advance, and that's as it should be. Using a social network like Facebook, birthday reminders are just one by-product of making the friend relationship explicit.

That's a good start, but Facebook is just one web site. I have friends (and, obviously, relatives) who are not on Facebook, nor should they have to be. What I really want is a personal assistant that goes to *all* the various sites, finds my friends and relatives, learns their birthdays, and tells me whose birthday is coming up.

I can't blame my stepmother for not friending me on Facebook — we're not at the point where everyone puts his personal information online and makes it pullable. But someday, when a child is born, her information will go online in her **online birth certificate** (Chapter 7), and that will be the authoritative source for her birth information. It will be incorporated into her personal **online data locker** (Chapter 9), and she'll pull reminders for her friends' and family members' birthdays, from there. And, as we'll see shortly, birthdays are just the tip of a huge information iceberg.

What Is Pulling?

Pulling represents the first change in how we use information in over 4,000 years. Some of the earliest written documents were records of transactions, showing how many camels were traded for how many rations of grain, etc. During the Industrial Revolution, companies developed **paper forms** for recording business data. When Edwin G. Seibels invented the filing cabinet in 1898, all those forms finally had a place to live. In the intervening eleven decades, including the past four decades of the computer revolution, that model hasn't changed. We still document what happens in the real world and then store the documents in virtual filing cabinets. The web itself has been a revolution in speed, scale, and availability of information, but not in *kind*. It seems every time I need to learn something online, it's in a PDF I need to download and read or a long Wikipedia article. We're still following behind our business processes, entering information into forms (think of the last time you went to see your doctor). We're still making copies of documents and emailing them as attachments. We're still managing all our files on our computer "desktops," complete with "folders" and "trash cans." In short, we are still moving everything by hand, the clumsy old-fashioned way, but now we use a mouse as our data pitchfork.

Pulling is different. When we pull information, we automatically get what we need when we need it. For example, today you send me a package by putting my physical address on it. Essentially, you are pushing the package to me, guessing I will be home to receive it. In the world of pull, you drop the package into the mail with my identifier on it, and I *pull the package to me,* wherever I am at the time (Chapter 8).

As we'll see, the world of pull is vastly more efficient than what we have today, and it leads to the performance economy (Chapter 16). I estimate conservatively that just implementing half of what I envision in this book will delete $1 trillion in waste from our economy. And it's all about how we handle a certain kind of information, called metadata.

What Is Metadata?

Metadata describes a thing or a person or a service. Examples of metadata include receipts, business cards, x-rays, menus, maps, patient charts, invoices, owner's manuals, etc. Brochures and catalogs are metadata. Your calendar and passport are metadata. The only thing that isn't metadata is **content**. A review of a particular wine is metadata, while an essay about that wine is content. Is a photo of your child content? If you took it to document your child's growth or haircut, it's metadata, but if you took it to enjoy, it's content. It could easily be both.

These days, digital photos have their own **format metadata** that records the date, time, exposure, file name, and other information into something called an exchangeable image file format (EXIF) file that helps you sort and work with your photos on your computer. All digital cameras use this standard format, which is governed by the Japan Electronics and Information Technology Industries Association.*

Photos also need a way to describe **content metadata**. Online photos will be semantic when they come with fields that say who or what is in them, where they are, the name of the event, and what the people are doing. To become part of the semantic web, those fields will need to be visible to and understood by search engines. We'll encounter much more metadata as we explore its uses throughout this book.

---

* Interestingly, the web site, exif.org, is not maintained by the consortium, but rather by a fan of the format!

What Is the Semantic Web?

Another word for semantic is **unambiguous**. In the semantic web, we declare what we mean in precise, standardized terms. *Data that is semantic means exactly the same thing to any system or person who uses it.*

The grocery store of the future and the automated supply chain behind it are part of the semantic web. They are becoming more real every day. The semantic web will realign our supply chains around the data that pulls the products through, rather than pushing them using the old supply chain mind-set. As we'll see in Chapter 4, the key to this transition isn't the cart – it's the availability of the information in a format the cart can understand and an information supply chain that tracks the information all the way from supplier to retailer, and even in the appliances at home. This new information infrastructure has already started in the United States and is spreading rapidly from retail to health care to financial reporting to research to transportation. Everything is going semantic, and the end result of making our metadata semantic is that it shifts our world from pushing information to pulling.

The semantic web tries to **make sense of written and spoken language** that we intuitively understand but computers normally don't. This is usually qualitative information, like reviews, opinions, descriptions, directions, and definitions.

In the semantic web, we make explicit the **underlying structure** of information. A form is a structured document. So is a contract, a business card, a catalog, a restaurant menu, an insurance policy, or a sales listing for an office building. Semantic software can recognize concept, relationship, parts, and whole.

The semantic web **specifies context** explicitly, using languages that give meaning to terms like "requires," "is similar to," "belongs to," etc. The context of a joint venture could be expressed explicitly, with each party expected to contribute its own information as the project goes along. The activities of a bank with a high loan-to-asset ratio could be monitored differently from a bank with a low ratio.

In the semantic web, the data allows us to **make inferences** and **draw conclusions**. For example, if Paul works for Frank and Frank works for Judy, then Paul works for Judy. Semantic reasoners draw conclusions like this from billions of individual assertions.

One of the primary goals of the semantic web is to **reuse data**. So the name and address you give to your insurance company goes straight to your doctor, and then transfers to the specialist, the lab, and the hospital. If you change your address, all these systems update simultaneously.

The semantic web **puts most resources online**, where many different systems use them in different ways, as needed. Also called "cloud computing" and "the open web," these online resources will change all industries, including yours.

In the semantic web, **we make everything findable by giving it a unique name**. In this book we'll see many examples of industries agreeing on a common name space and common definitions for terms to make everyone much more productive.

The Semantic Web

In computer science, the term "semantic" refers to the meaning of a word or phrase. The words "couch" and "sofa" refer to the same thing – two different words that have the same underlying semantic meaning. When I use the word "semantic" in this book, I mean the unambiguous underlying meaning of a term. I specifically don't imply any kind of artificial intelligence or "smart" programming behind the scenes. I simply mean **unambiguous** – understood by all people and all software to mean the same thing.

In the 1990s, Sir Tim Berners-Lee coined the term "semantic web" to mean a **web of data** that interconnects and can be reused over and over, forming databases that live online, rather than in incompatible database "silos" buried inside various web sites.

The semantic web uses **adaptive systems** that go far beyond traditional programming or artificial intelligence. As our systems learn more, they will get smarter and keep up with us. As they gather the semantic exhaust of our actions and transactions, our systems will make us far more productive. As Nova Spivack of Radar Networks explains in his blog *Minding the Planet*:

> *A lot of people have been working on making the software smarter.*
> *In the semantic web, we're going to start making the data smarter.*

The Semantic Web Acid Test

When looking at any particular solution, there is a two-question test to see if it's really part of the semantic web:

1. **Is it semantic?** That is, are the terms unambiguous and tagged in a royalty-free format, governed by a nonprofit organization, that all software programs can understand? For the purposes of this book, I don't use the term "semantic" for information that is in a proprietary or in-house format that isn't widely used and must be translated from one system to another.

2. **Is it on the web?** Is it online using a common name space that makes it easily findable? Is it shared among collaborators or companies? Does it use the information already online to get smarter as more people use the system?

We'll apply this test many times in this book, so you can see for yourself where different industries are and how much more they have to do.*

---

*Some technologists feel that semantic web data *must* be expressed using a language called RDF. I disagree. I believe simple, unambiguous formats are part of the semantic web.

Let's take bowling as an example. **Is the scoring system sematic?** Yes. The scoring system is extremely precise, and a strike means a strike to any software system that sees this piece of data. Is that really true? No, it's not. Today's bowling systems are proprietary and the data is internal to the system. League organizers still write all the scores down by hand after each game. So even though the system captures information unambiguously, it doesn't meet our criteria of shareability and commonality. Put a no here, but give them credit for generating scores automatically. **Is it on the web?** Not yet. You can't see your score online after your game, and you can't compile all your scores as you go, building a web of bowling-history information as a natural result of going bowling at different places. League organizers publish scores online, but only as results for humans to read, not as data for your software agent to pick up. Another no.

Let's look at travel. **Are your airline miles semantic?** They are unambiguous, but they are in a proprietary format that is not transferrable to other systems. **Are they on the web?** Do all your miles go into an online data locker where you can see your trip details just by getting on airplanes and flying? Yes. Are they portable and combinable with other airlines? No. Can these miles be used by all systems and reused in other contexts? Are they connected to your expense reports? Does the expense report get generated automatically, as a by-product of your getting on an airplane and flying somewhere? Once again, no. All your travel data is in some proprietary web site for each airline, with a different log-in for each one, and if you want to construct a map of your trips or report your expenses, you have to do it manually without making any use of the data that already exists but is locked in a data silo (database).

We'll see a few examples where both answers are yes in this book, but not many. Applying the semantic web acid test shows you how far most industries have yet to go.

The Dvorak Key Layout

In 1868, Christopher Sholes patented the typewriter. Initially, he arranged the keys alphabetically, since people already knew the alphabet. Once a typist got up to speed, however, he found that many words, like "deal," caused the mechanical keys to become tangled, because the *d* and the *e* came from almost the same angle. Sholes studied the problem and, in 1878, was granted a patent on the QWERTY layout, putting the keys for often-typed English words in *difficult-to-reach* places, favoring the left hand, and leaving *less common letters* under the resting fingers. Sholes's aim was to **slow the typist down**, so the keys were less likely to get tangled, speeding up typing overall. That clever trick worked until electronic typewriters and then computers adopted the same keyboard. Sholes would be dismayed to learn that his 1878 keyboard is now sold over 200 million times every year.[3]

In 1936, August Dvorak devised and patented a much more effective layout for typing. The Dvorak keyboard put the most common consonants under the right hand – where words often start and end – and common vowels under the left hand. A few facts about the Dvorak versus the QWERTY layout:

> In typical English, 70 percent of letters occur in the home row in Dvorak, compared to 31 percent in QWERTY.

> The error rate for QWERTY typists of the same ability is about twice that of Dvorak typists.

> The word TYPEWRITER was designed into the top row of the QWERTY keyboard for salespeople to use as an easy demonstration word.

> A study by the U.S. Navy showed they could recover the costs of retraining their typists in Dvorak in ten days.

> The average beginner typist requires 56 hours of training to attain a speed of 40 words per minute in QWERTY; in Dvorak, the time is 18 hours.[4]

> Most computers have Dvorak layouts as an option.

Better standards will make us vastly more efficient in almost everything we do, and the Dvorak layout is another good example. A better standard than QWERTY exists but most people are unaware of it. In my experience, it takes two to three weeks to get up to speed on the Dvorak layout, typing a little slower at first but then typing faster forever after.[5] You can switch the layout on your computer today and learn a system that will save you time in the long run. Will you? Are you willing to invest the time to learn a new, more efficient way to type, realizing that you've been tricked into using an outdated, inefficient standard all these years? When you finish reading this book, I hope you'll look at your QWERTY keyboard as part of the problem, not part of the solution.

3: The Shipper Project

Pull Concept: Changing to a Customer-Centered View

> *Metadata is worldview; sorting is a political act.*
>
> – Clay Shirky

TO START US THINKING about the management shift in going from push to pull, I'll describe a project that doesn't exist and ask interested readers to help me get it started. Companies that ship packages generally have to deal with the U.S. Postal Service (USPS), UPS, or FEDEX. Rather than competing with vendor lock-in using proprietary tracking numbers and message formats, these carriers could switch to a new set of open formats that will bring their industry into the twenty-first century. The goals of the project are to give shippers more flexibility, seamlessly link shipping and freight, reduce returns, and save resources. Let's start by understanding the world of carriers and how they see their customers.

Note: In this industry, a **shipper** is a company with parcels (packages) to ship, and a **carrier** is a company that delivers parcels.

Owning the Customer

In the 1980s, IBM shipped machines and parts all around the country. At each shipping department, a clerk first chose a carrier, then filled out a form called a waybill that included all the details of shipping, handling, and charges. If the company shipped 100 parcels, the clerk filled out 100 waybills. A few days later, the company received an invoice for each individual shipment. In 1986, IBM shipped more than 17,000 packages a day and actually paid more than 17,000 separate invoices every single day, just for shipping.[6]

Using computers, companies became more productive. They could now store their own addresses, use mailing lists to print out their paper waybills, and consolidate billing. This was so effective that the carriers began installing proprietary computer systems for generating paperwork – Airborne Express Libra, Federal Express Powership, and UPS Maxiship. Companies like IBM started hiring computer science graduate students to keep all their systems, software, and codes up to date.

Today, as this $90 billion industry consolidates, the few carriers left have even more power, and the proprietary "solutions" continue to dig deeper and deeper into the shippers' IT departments. As an example, one of the biggest shippers in the country is Dell. In 2006, Dell shipped 20.5 million personal computers domestically, virtually all of them via UPS.[7] According to Jerry Hempstead, a shipping consultant, if a UPS driver attempted to deliver a Dell system and the recipient refused it, the UPS driver entered a message that went to a special Dell call center almost immediately. The call center would then call the customer and offer a discount to accept the system. More than half the time, the customer would change his or her mind and agree to take the system (the call center was empowered to take up to $200 off the original price, depending on the system). Another message would go immediately to the same UPS driver, who would drive back and deliver the computer before the customer changed his or her mind. Sometimes it was just a matter of ten or fifteen minutes later.

This is a win for UPS, which spends more money each year developing, maintaining, and acquiring technology than it spends on trucks.[8] Its custom data solutions make it harder for clients to switch carriers. Yet, in 2007, UPS "fired" Dell, handing FEDEX the business, claiming the account wasn't profitable enough.[9] In this world, the carrier with the most leverage over the client wins. If you work at UPS, you see the world this way:

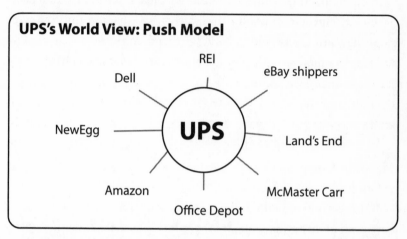

UPS's World View: Push Model

REI
Dell
eBay shippers
NewEgg — **UPS** — Land's End
Amazon
McMaster Carr
Office Depot

UPS uses proprietary data formats to link all its customers, improving efficiency as its network grows. Many "solutions" are one-off implementations.

Both UPS and FEDEX have this same company-centered view of the customer, trying to build *more* barriers to prevent clients from switching, shaving the last percent of efficiency out of established processes.

The Power Shift

Like the restaurant owner who doesn't own his freezers or refrigerators, shippers have gotten used to integrating their systems with carriers' proprietary "solutions." That's the way push works, and it will end when shippers realize they deserve better. They should be at the center.

Using the pull approach, all carriers switch to the same data standards to track shipments, from Johannesburg to Jackson Hole. Using a new universal tracking number and open standards for messaging creates *package-level autonomy*: the package itself will send a message to the customer to make sure he or she is there to receive it. Dell can then add, subtract, and combine carriers easily – something it could never do before. Dell can compare carriers based on their performance and let the system choose the right carrier for each individual shipment.

Smaller shippers can now use the same software big companies use, aggregating medium-size and small shippers with software that lives online and runs in a browser with no installation costs. Now all companies have access to the same interconnected web of shipping data.

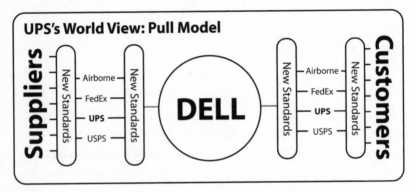

Using common data standards, UPS sees all carriers as part of an integrated solution built around the customer's shipping and logistics needs.

In the pull era, we'll go from a single carrier at the center of the universe to a shipper like Dell at the center. If you work at UPS, your new business vision has your customers at the center; this puts UPS side by side with its competitors. **In the world of pull, you don't own the customer; the customer owns you.**

In this scenario, UPS, USPS, and FEDEX are now partners, whether they like it or not.* They can start to cooperate on delivering packages while competing fiercely for the relationships using the quality of their services, not their proprietary systems. They can drop the expensive

---

*To some degree, they already are. FEDEX has a long-term contract with USPS to handle its air parcel business from airport to airport.

duplication of services in the last mile, where the U.S. Postal Service is often superior. They can trade credits for making each other more efficient. They can start to connect to the freight system and better coordinate international deliveries with foreign carriers who adopt the same standards. In this future, a factory in Cambodia addresses each item in a container to its proper final destination and everything is pulled through. By moving the metadata, the physical goods travel through the system and can be rerouted easily on the go, without warehouse and distribution middlemen causing delays.

Critical Mass

The project is aimed at companies that ship more than about fifty packages to fifty addresses per day. The idea is to replace the proprietary formats with a new **universal tracking number** that includes the carrier name as one of the data elements and a new set of standards all carriers can use to put shippers back in control of their shipments. At first, this is in addition to all the proprietary bar codes and data formats, but eventually it will replace them.

It makes no sense to sit down with UPS, FEDEX, and the USPS and ask them nicely to conform to a set of universal shipping standards. Instead, we'll build new standards from the bottom up, the way many semantic web standards are built, and we'll make the case that the new standards are better for everyone in the long run. First, we'll start an online discussion group among parcel shippers and plot our strategy together. The group of early volunteers will define the core use cases that drive the requirements. We'll need standards for bar codes, messaging, routing, reporting, billing, etc. Fortunately, there are nonprofits set up to deliver these kinds of standards – for services, businesses, even shipping. We'll make the standards open and extendable – to allow for more innovation in the future. We'll design a schedule for development and testing. Then we'll set up a pilot project to give more shippers confidence that this new process can save them money. With enough shippers on board, the pilot project may make the carriers realize that this approach is in their best interest as well.

If the vendor-centered diagram reminds you of your industry, all it takes to change to a customer-centered view is a critical mass of customers who want to save money and get radically better service. When enough motivated customers get behind something, they can surprise a lot of push-based marketing people who think they have their customers by the throat. In the long run, even the carriers will benefit as they will adapt much more swiftly to new customer demands and find new customers their old, proprietary standards didn't give them access to.

If your company ships more than fifty parcels a day, ask your shipping manager to find out more about this project at **ThePowerofPull.com**.

What's Next

In the first phase of this project, we'll learn to ship the package by first shipping the data, using the new open standards. As the data moves, so moves the package (in contrast with the way it's done today). Then we're going to learn to ship the package by *not* shipping the data – keeping the data in one place and letting the messages pull each package to its destination. We'll learn how to do many of these things in later chapters.

4: Retail Pull

Pull Concept: From Supply Chain to Pull Chain

> *Today's retail model is struggling. It's still largely a system built for the realities of an earlier era – a linear, push-based process where products are manufactured in isolation and put into market en masse from factory to truck to store, for customers who do the majority of their shopping in suburban malls. . . . Today, this system is straining to adapt to global supply chains, new ways and venues for selling – both physical and virtual – and a very different kind of consumer.*
>
> – IBM white paper

I'M WALKING INTO THE METRO GROUP'S TEST-MARKET RETAIL STORE in Tönisvorst, outside Düsseldorf in Germany's northern Rhineland. Metro uses this megastore in a sleepy suburb that primarily serves retired people to test their new electronic supply chain and other technology innovations. (If retired people can figure it out, anyone can.)

I'm here to see the smart cart – the one I imagined ten years ago in my book *Futurize Your Enterprise*. As I always envisioned it, while shopping, you would put your items into a cart, which would then display your shopping list, preferences, contents of the cart, coupons, total, bank balance, etc. That's what the Metro Group thought, too, until they realized that "logging in" to a shopping cart was going to be more difficult than using your own phone. The carts here are normal shopping carts. On your way in, you stop at a counter, and an employee installs the store's shopping application on your mobile phone. If you don't have a phone, you can borrow one of theirs.

Now, using the camera on my phone, I scan the bar code on any product or shelf to see pricing, find more information on the product, and get custom offers. I add the item to my cart, say how many I'm getting, and my phone shows my cart's inventory and total. I can also add an item to a future wish list or use the bar codes at home to build a shopping list.

Using the bar codes is surprisingly easy. When it's time to check out, I can either scan the items myself or let the phone add everything up. A friendly woman sits at a desk to let me know she's there to help, but otherwise she doesn't intrude. Now I can swipe my credit/debit card and key in my PIN or use my established account and pay directly by phone. Or I can pay by fingerprint, which has proved surprisingly popular, especially with parents.

While consumers use bar codes to scan and manage individual items, the store is one of the first in the world to use RFID – radio-frequency identification – tags to track individual products. All the fresh meat and fish packages get RFID tags put on at the same time they have their bar code and price put on. Then they are displayed in a "smart cooler." When I take a package out, the cooler knows which piece of inventory has just left. The system tracks sales of various products by exact time of day, orders replacement packages, and tells the clerk which packages are out of date and must be removed.

During my visit in 2008, the RFID tags cost about 10 euro-cents each. The cost of processing and managing the information is also 10 euro-cents per tag, so the company spends 20 euro-cents to tag and manage each package. For a steak or anything more expensive, the economics work – the company finds the information more valuable than the cost.

The bar codes are an interim strategy. When RFIDs become cheap enough, most items in the store will have them. At that point, I expect the cart will have an RFID scanner, and it will relay the information to your phone. The phone will likely be the primary display for seeing your purchases, managing lists, making a payment, etc. Your phone will automatically track items as you put them into or take them out of your cart. (Bring your own bags and put items into your bags right in the cart for a quick getaway.) Metro Group's goal is to make stacking everything on the conveyor belt "a thing of the past."

The RFID Demonstration Center

A short €100 taxi ride away, in Neuss, I have the pleasure of taking a tour of the RFID innovation center. In the "House of the Future" exhibit, every appliance has a display. I take a bottle of Riesling out of the wine fridge, and the inventory shows one bottle fewer. I take a jar of pickles out of the refrigerator, and if I don't put it back by the next morning, it will update my personal shopping list. Putting a pair of jeans from the laundry basket into the washing machine gives a nice surprise – the washing machine display lists its contents and warns me when I put something in that should only be dry-cleaned.

The demonstration center shows how embedding RFIDs in the floor can help autonomous robots navigate a factory. It also shows a new kind of carpet that has RFID tags embedded and a "smart" vacuum cleaner that always stays on the carpet, following the tags.

In the warehouse, an automated rack system sorts clothing for distribution to different locations. Each item of clothing has its own RFID tag, and the system knows its final destination. In just a few seconds, the system sorts hundreds of items into five different lines, waiting to be put on trucks to different locations. This is at least twenty times faster (and more accurate) than sorting by hand. Of course, the magic continues at the retailer, where each item knows where it belongs in the store.*

Galeria Kaufhof

Another €100 taxi ride and I'm at the Galeria Kaufhof store in Essen. Here on the men's floor, about 30,000 items have been RFID-tagged. There are RFID readers everywhere, even in the dressing rooms, where you can see a "virtual you" in as many outfits as you like, just by holding the clothing up to the display. The display shows you colors, sizes, and stock on hand.

There are various "magic mirrors" on the floor that show what sizes are in stock and makes suggestions for putting an outfit together (some call this the "virtual wife" feature). The best part for me was taking an armload of shirts and pants to the cash register. I just dropped the pile of products on the counter and the display showed the item list and total instantly.

This store actually works. The warehouses really are connected, and the information goes all the way back to the manufacturers. It's still a learning environment, but more vendors are coming on board all the time.

Standards for Retail

The **Universal Product Code** – the bar code on all the items you buy at the grocery store – has grown into a worldwide standard for electronic identification of:

---

*Want to take this tour yourself? Just go to **future-store.org** and watch the excellent videos. More stores will soon be launching in select German cities, and the supply chain is gearing up (slowly) to support it.

Containers

Pallets

Cases

SKUs*

Products

Since its introduction in 1974, the UPC has identified about 5 billion items for more than 1 million companies in more than 140 countries. According to GS1, the consortium that oversees the standard and allocates the codes, the UPC has saved consumers and businesses over $1 trillion worldwide.[10]

GS1 also issues RFID tags using codes that correspond to the bar codes. RFID tags come in all sizes, from the size of a grain of sand, to a glass ampoule the size of a grain of rice that can be injected under the skin, to a flat sticker about the size of a pocket comb or a business card. They can be stuck on any surface. RFID tags are cheap because they are passive – the reader device sends a signal and the reader reads the signal the tag reflects back. Today, RFIDs (which I pronounce "arfids") are tracking vacuum cleaners, flat-screen TVs, printers, patients in hospitals, bottles of pills, driver's licenses, car tires, pets, razor blades, and DVDs.

Because of the high price of tags and infrastructure, most tags at the product level are on expensive or critical items, like medical devices, blood, organs, etc. There are service-level tags for ski passes or race numbers. In Europe, DHL and IBM have already built a "cold chain" for shipping drugs that provides real-time temperature readings from active tags and can stop a shipment at the next checkpoint if a drug's temperature goes out of range.

And that's the power of retail pull: when a consumer takes an item

---

*An SKU is a stock-keeping unit. This can be a box with several small products or it can be a single product.

off a shelf, she is actually pulling on the entire supply chain, right down through the distributors and manufacturers to the companies that supply all the parts and services along the way. So the retail purchase is just the tip of a huge information iceberg, and the payoff comes when everyone is in synch. Soon, RFID tags will be so cheap that many products will have not one but many – reflecting all the different suppliers of all the parts.

It's more than just physical tags. We're building an entire **metadata supply chain,** with scanners, software, smart shelves, software tags for new data formats, and more. The Metro Group and others – like Wal-Mart and Wegmans in the United States – are leading the way, showing that the investment can pay off and the added benefits are tremendous.

Active Tags

RFID tags are passive – they reflect a number back when scanned. Active tags, like the new and exciting RUBEE-standard tags, have a small battery and act like a tiny switching device on a network. RUBEE tags are more autonomous – they can pass signals along a chain or form a mesh network that creates ad hoc smart environments. RUBEE tags can transmit information farther and through more materials than RFID. Today, RUBEE tags are tracking high-value items like livestock, medical devices, organs and blood products, hazardous chemicals, guns, gemstones, and people. Tomorrow, a network of RUBEE chips can track a herd of cattle on a ranch, manage cars in traffic, help teams pass messages in difficult environments, and much more. A shipment of goods can "keep in touch" with each other, and if they get too far apart or too close, they can report suspected damage during shipment.

Catalog Synchronization

Companies that send products to large retailers like Target and Wal-Mart now feed their product-description data into the Global Data

Synchronization Network (GDSN) from GS1. GDSN is a catalog synchronization system that goes all the way through the supply chain, from producer to retailer. If you're a supplier to a large retailer, you can publish a GDSN version of your catalog, and that information will scream through the supply chain in seconds. Data registries aggregate many feeds into a single master catalog automatically. Add a new product to your catalog, and it's visible to thousands of retailers by next morning. Change a price and that change will make it around the world in less than forty-eight hours.

GDSN now powers over 5 billion transactions a day.[11] The standards are open, but the program involves certification and extreme attention to accurate metadata. Using GDSN, Wal-Mart has decreased item maintenance from fifteen days to one. Wal-Mart now requires GDSN data from all its suppliers. Wegmans, a chain of over seventy grocery stores, has more than 80 percent of its trading partners now sending synchronized data through the GDSN. Order productivity is up 50 percent. Shipping costs are down by $3.5 million per year.

You have to pull suppliers into this kind of program, and the magic starts when more than a few of them come on board. Because of nonprofits like GS1, data now flies through this channel, and the faster it goes the better.

Master Data Management

GDSN is an example of a master data management scheme. Master data refers to nontransactional reference data, like descriptions and prices. Once the systems are in place, you need to focus on the three keys to success in managing a master data supply chain:

1. Accuracy of data

2. Accuracy of data

3. Accuracy of data

To help improve the quality of data used across the GDSN, the members of GS1 built a data quality management system to validate the existence and effectiveness of key data management business processes. Once this was in place, Wegmans found it no longer needed to scan and reconcile items at the back door – it switched to a spot-check system and went from forty minutes per week per store to around twenty minutes per week per store. Wegmans saved 7 percent in receiving costs by switching to the spot-check system. This savings alone should pay for the data integrity effort, which then pays huge dividends as the data flows throughout the chain. Most large stores in Europe have been using inexpensive LCD price tags on the shelves for years, showing current prices on each item without having to apply stickers.

As one consultant explained to me, "We can now drive our data at ten times the speed we used to, and we can also drive our mistakes through the supply chain at the same rate." This chain is as strong as its weakest link. To reap the benefits of synchronization, you need to spend more of your time making sure the original data is worth syndicating.

Spime

What will consumers do when they get their RFID-tagged products home? Plenty. I'm going to use a term coined by Bruce Sterling, fiction author and techno visionary. Spime (space + time) is anything personal that's findable or manageable by its metadata. Who needs to categorize? Put your books anywhere – on any shelf or under the bed. Later, just look them up by name and find them using an inexpensive RFID scanner. You can add RFIDs to your jewelry, sunglasses, and pets, so you can identify what's yours, or your phone can beep if you leave the tennis club without your racquet. Anything with GPS capability can tell you where it is or where it's been. Spime is how your washing machine knows you've just put a red shirt in along with your white sheets.

If the interior of your car is approaching the melting point for the chocolates you just bought, the chocolates will tell your car, and your car will send you a text message. You'll respond by starting it and turning on the air conditioner right from your phone. If you leave your reading glasses on the train, how will you find them? Simple. Just wait. In a few minutes, you'll get a message from someone saying where they are. Today, you can go to eyeglassrescue.com and get a sleeve to put on your eyeglasses that has a unique ID number and a phone number to call for a reward. Want to sign up for similar services for everything you own? I didn't think so. In the pull era, *everything you own* will have a single identifier, eliminating the middleman, turning it into trackable, findable spime.

Consumers will get many other benefits from keeping their RFID tags active after purchase. In the future, your refrigerator will adjust its temperature to the needs of its contents, using less energy when you have pickles and mustard but cooling down when it sees a package of raw meat. You'll ask your kitchen what can be made with the ingredients it has on hand, and you'll query your neighbor (with permission) to see if he has the cup of sugar you need for your cake.

Spime isn't science fiction – it's already part of the pull way of using information.* We may not have many consumer-level RFIDs yet, but in ten years we'll take them for granted. You'll go online and see all your stuff laid out on a map – a map of the world, if necessary.

> ### The Sticking Point

RFID is great for getting goods where they need to go. RFID helps retailers like Wal-Mart, Tesco, and American Apparel in dozens of ways,

---

* See consumer solutions at **widetag.com** and industrial-strength solutions at **spime.com**. And, just for fun, visit **w-41.com**.

using tags on containers, pallets, and rolling cages. For now, they are letting bar codes do the work at the product level, but it's a small step from here to include RFIDs on each product.

Manufacturers and suppliers resist electronic tagging (putting RFIDs on) at any level, because it doesn't benefit them. They only do it if the retailer requires it. They complain that tagging products and managing the extra metadata is too costly, and they get nothing from it.

Another reason manufacturers aren't jumping is that RFIDs still need work. Today's scanners have trouble seeing all the tags – the error rates are too high. Seeing one tag on a pallet is fairly easy. Registering 144 tags on all the products on each pallet every time is much harder – the tags can be obscured by packaging, other products, and other objects. At the moment, the semantic metadata supply chain is broken at its weakest link – the manufacturers. I predict that will change, for four important reasons:

Reason 1: Bar codes. All manufacturers eventually adopted the UPC bar code, and they make more money as a result. It lets manufacturers build their catalogs around a common standard. It means easier checkout. It means more automation and fewer errors. The RFID is a new, more accessible version of the UPC. While the UPC will continue to be adequate for low-cost items, RFIDs will soon be cheap enough and accurate enough to have significant advantages over bar codes.

Reason 2: Improvement. Many companies lose sales because the product isn't on the shelf – wouldn't you like to see an accurate count of all your products on all your reseller's shelves right from your laptop, so you can know what's really on the shelf at any given time? The Galleria Kaufhof project showed that a business case can be made for a large clothing manufacturer whose products are made in Asia and sold in Europe. Four pilot companies estimated return on investment (ROI) at two to three years, with the main benefits being reduced errors and improved sales as a result of more accurate product placement in the store.[12] The details matter, and the cost per tag is a critical element in the ROI calculation. Their report predicted that the early adopters will be store-branded items that are relatively expensive (for example, a house brand of suits and jackets), because in that case the retailer is willing to pay to have the tags put on and track its goods from the moment they leave the factory. R&D is exploding; there are many new designs for RFIDs and the systems that pull them through. Prices are coming down as each application finds a winning reason to exist.

Reason 3: Price. Not only is the price coming down, but the cost of managing the metadata will come down as well. When tags have their own power supply, they'll register more easily. All the tools and supplies will come down to a price where the early majority will start piling in. In a few years, we'll start building the chips and antennae into our products – weaving them, molding them, casting them – so there won't be an extra tagging step. The products will come off the line tied semantically to their online birth certificates (Chapter 7) and everyone will use the metadata from beginning to end.

Reason 4: Upstream pull. If you're a farmer selling salad mix, why do you need all that fancy radio technology? Because your customer wants to know that the salad never goes above 44 degrees Fahrenheit and isn't out of date. You either tag or you're off the shelf. If you make running shoes, you're going to learn that your competitor just started putting RFIDs in all its shoes, and they are flying off the shelves because runners want to register for races using the unique number associated with their shoes and track all their results in one place. If you make eyeglasses, your customers will want to find their lost glasses using the RFID scanner that just came with their spime-enabled mobile phone. If you sell wine, your customers will demand it so they can track their inventory in their RFID-enabled wine cellar. If you make office machines, you'll tag them so your customers can better manage their facilities and repairs. You can do it now, or you can do it later, but eventually you'll start tagging individual products.

What's Next

When all this plumbing gets hooked up, customers will pull products through the supply chain, rather than the other way around. It's less about the specific technology and more about changing the way we think about our customers and their roles in our businesses.

Will every item in the store eventually have an RFID tag? I think it will. We'll see them on perishables, even on individual avocados, because the smarter the perishable supply chain is, the higher its margins, and margins are razor-thin to start with. What about something small and cheap, like a box of toothpicks? Even though it's not cost-efficient to put RFIDs on small cheap items, it's the only way to eliminate the cashier and the clumsy scanning process at checkout. The self-service bar code readers they installed aren't cutting it. Most of us pump our own gas; in a few years, we'll check ourselves out of the grocery store simply by walking out the front door.

The RFID ecosystem closes the time gap between what happens to products and when we know it. Talk with your customers about shortening the distance from one end to the other. Real-time information saves money in ways you can't even count when you don't have it.

5: Financial Transparency

Pull Concept: Taxonomies

> *The effect that* XBRL *will have on the business community will be more significant than the transition from paper and pencil analysis of financial information to the use of electronic spreadsheets.*
>
> – Mike Willis, founding chairman of XBRL International, PWC partner

WHATEVER THE CAUSE OF THE GREAT DEPRESSION, which started in October 1929, there's no disagreement that one of the solutions to the problem was Franklin Roosevelt's creation of the Securities Act of 1933 and the Securities Exchange Act of 1934. These laws created the Security and Exchange Commission, whose first chairman, Joseph P. Kennedy, required public companies to file financial statements and make them public.

Today, the SEC oversees the seven major laws affecting the U.S. securities industry, all of which were designed in response to various market and moral crises. The failure of the SEC to protect investors from disasters at Enron, Tyco, Bear Stearns, Fanny Mae, Lehman Brothers, and many others shows conclusively that trying to update and enforce the 1933 laws is a failed strategy.

In 2008, financial markets reeled from a toxic cocktail of greed, shortsightedness, outdated rulemaking, structural bias, and hidden details. Part of the solution to the problem, one that will help reduce the mismatch between markets and reality, will be increased transparency. Fortunately, the tool we need for better transparency is already here. XBRL, the EXtensible Business Reporting Language, will play a big role in the stabilization of stock and credit markets worldwide. In this chapter, I'll introduce you to this game-changing standard that will accelerate the arrival of a pull-based financial system.

The Test Pilot

In 1947, when Chuck Yeager became the first man to break the sound barrier, Harold Hoffman was a weather forecaster in the U.S. Air Force. He was so impressed with the flying ace's feat that, ten years later, he named his first son Charles. Little did he know that Charles Hoffman, who now goes by Charlie, would have a small but very important role to play in the future of our economy. Charlie would become the test pilot for an idea that will form the foundation of corporate financial reporting.

Back in the 1950s, if you wanted to look at a corporation's financial records, you had to go in person to an SEC reading room. If you wanted a document, you put in a request and the SEC would make copies for you. In the 1970s, photocopiers allowed the reading rooms to fulfill requests much faster. Since 1996, these same reports have been available in EDGAR, the SEC's online database, and displayed as web pages, so anyone could browse them easily. To use the information, analysts employ people to re-enter the data into their own custom-built databases. EDGAR was, and still is, an online filing cabinet for documents meant for people to print and read.

In 1998, Charlie, then a CPA with a head for using software to reduce the drudgery of accounting, had an idea. He thought it might be helpful to create a standard, computer-readable format for business financial reports, with a standard name for each field, so when one software system passes a report to another, each can understand the information instantly.

What happened next was so unusual in the world of accounting that Charlie remembers it vividly: "I knew this guy Wayne Harding at Great Plains. Wayne happened to be the chairman of one of the committees of the American Institute of Certified Public Accountants (AICPA). He said I should present my idea at their next meeting. It started at 8 A.M. I taught them a bit about XML* and the idea of creating a standard format for financial results, and I was done by 10 A.M. By noon, we had a pilot project sketched out. Two weeks later, Wayne said they gave him $50,000 to cover expenses. The accounting firm I was working at agreed to allow me to work on the project full time, and XBRL was born."

XBRL was a good idea from the beginning, but it wasn't easy to communicate to accountants. "My strategy," Charlie says, "was to take away all the possible reasons for them to say no. If I tried to explain XML, it wouldn't work. Many business people can't think abstractly, and most technical people can't think concretely enough. So I had to switch hats when talking with accountants. Instead of showing them something new, I showed them what they have today – a spreadsheet that looked like a financial report. They could understand that." Underneath, the XBRL document was a very carefully structured set of machine-readable formats and terms. Charlie then built a separate style sheet that rendered it like a normal financial statement. A computer program could read it without the style sheet and get the data unambiguously.

By July 1999, Charlie and his team had built a number of prototypes. By October of that year, people from the big accounting firms and large software vendors joined the XBRL steering committee. By 2000, XBRL International was a global organization helping governments around

---

* XML, the extensible markup language, is the fundamental language on which XBRL (and many other standards mentioned in this book), is based.

the world build XBRL into their reporting requirements. In the United States, Charlie and a group of CPAs and technical people hammered out the XBRL 1.0 specification and a dictionary of about 2,000 terms for financial reporting. Many companies in the United States started using XBRL *voluntarily*. By 2004, some thirty countries had pilot projects going.

What Exactly Is XBRL?

XBRL is a language that lets you build a financial report using industry-standard terms and tags. The report may be rendered to look similar to the paper report it replaces, but in the report itself every number has a special tag that says what it is, and every term comes from a restricted vocabulary made for reporting. An XBRL document has three main parts:

The values are the numbers and words that make up the business information you are trying to report. Typically, the numbers come from some sort of business system, like a spreadsheet or enterprise resource planning (ERP) system whose data is mapped to the kind of report you want to create.

The tags are special names that come from a controlled vocabulary of precise accounting and reporting terms you might use in a report. Each value has a specific tag, and that tag connects to the term and its definition. One tag might be called CurrentFederalTaxExpense, another might be called TrucksSold.

The dictionary gives a precise (semantic) definition of each term in the vocabulary, including references and examples. The definitions come from laws, international standards, and written specifications.

The dictionary isn't actually included with the report – it's a reference document that lives online, where all people and all software can find it. If some of your business information needs a custom tag, there is a formal process for making and defining new tags. If your company sells motor vehicles, then you will have custom tags for categories like cars, trucks, fleet vehicles, parts, etc. The terms define what kind of value to expect – you can't enter text if the term requires a dollar amount. If a field can have several possible values other than a yes-no answer or a number, the values come from another **controlled vocabulary** (for example, the type of a loan or the type of corporate entity).

The XBRL dictionary is actually more than an alphabetical list of terms. The dictionary also specifies rules and structure. When a dictionary has a hierarchical structure, like an outline, it's called a **taxonomy**. The XBRL taxonomy is a group of hierarchies (tree structures) for different purposes, each with categories and subcategories at the branch points and tags at the "leaves" of the tree. The taxonomy says not only what the terms mean but also specifies the relationships between the terms (see figure: US GAAP Taxonomy).

A taxonomy can also encode rules. A taxonomy can specify that "Total Assets" is the sum of all the fields tagged as assets. A taxonomy can make sure a footnote includes its numerical values. XBRL now has dozens of predefined taxonomies that combine like Lego bricks to build a given pro forma report. As companies add new elements (categories, subcategories, and tags) to the taxonomy, the XBRL community encourages adopting the same names for the same thing, so reports stay comparable.

In XBRL, a report (for example, an income statement) is a tagged set of numbers and included notes. Once you've added the XBRL tags to your data, a program called an **XBRL processor** helps you create your report. The processor uses the rules in the taxonomy to make sure there are no errors. And the final document is called an **instance document** or, simply, a report.

An instance document and its taxonomy go hand in hand – if all companies submit annual reports using the same taxonomy, analysts can easily compare all elements of the reports across the board. If anyone changes the rules or extends the taxonomy, all the software adapts easily, because the taxonomy is included by reference.

Finally, if you want humans to read your XBRL report, you can apply a **style sheet** and use a special program called a **viewer**. You can apply any number of different style sheets, so the information comes out looking differently, or even in another language and currency. Any good XBRL viewer will let you see the definition of any term by letting you see the appropriate part of the online taxonomy.

US GAAP Taxonomy

US GAAP Taxonomy tree	LABELS		
⋮	**Role**	**Lang**	**Label**
⊞110201 - Statement - Statement of Financial Pos	Standard Label	en-US	**Preferred Stock Redemption Premium**
⊞112000 - Statement - Statement of Financial Pos			The excess of (1) fair value of the consideration transferred to the holders of the preferred stock over (2) the carrying amount of the preferred stock in the registrant's balance sheet, during the accounting period, which will be subtracted from net earnings to arrive at net earnings available to common shareholders in the calculation of earnings per share.
⊞124000 - Statement - Statement of Income (Incl			
⊟Income Statement [Abstract]			
⊟Statement [Table]	Documentation	en-US	
⊞Statement, Scenario [Axis]			
⊟Statement [Line Items]			
⊟Net Income (Loss) Available to Common S			
⊟Net Income (Loss) Attributable to Parent			
⊞Net Income (Loss), Including Portion Att	**REFERENCES**		
⊞Net Income (Loss) Attributable to Nonc	**Role**	**Reference**	
Net Income (Loss) Attributable to Par		Name	Emerging Issues Task Force (EITF)
⊟Preferred Stock Dividends and Other Adj	Presentation	Number	D-42
Preferred Stock Dividends		Publisher	FASB
Redeemable Preferred Stock Dividen		Name	Accounting Standards Codification
Convertible Preferred Stock Converte		Par	2
Preferred Stock Redemption Premiu		Publisher	FASB
Redeemable Preferred Stock Increase		Section	S99
General Partner Distributions		SubTopic	10
		Topic	260
		URI	http://asc.fasb.org/extlink&oid=637249

Browse the entire taxonomy at **viewer.xbrl.us**

The US GAAP taxonomy is a hierarchy of document categories and terms. Seen as a tree structure, the various statements are the trunks of the trees, and the tags are the leaves. Each term refers to its formal definition, defined by a governing or standards body.

The Turning Point

In 2005, Christopher Cox, chairman of the SEC, called Louis Matherne, who was then president of XBRL International, with an offer. Cox said he knew XBRL wasn't ready for the more than 700,000 reports filed with the SEC each year, but he wanted it to be, and he was ready to help. Cox created a new department of interactive data inside the SEC, with the vision of turning EDGAR into an online hub for financial reporting data. And he put together many of the key players who would take XBRL to the next level. In 2006, Cox announced that the SEC would spend $54 million to upgrade the EDGAR system and $5 million more on the taxonomies, to be built by XBRL US, under the international governing body, XBRL International.

XBRL International

More than 110 countries now use or require XBRL. Most European countries have voluntary filing programs, and many mandate the use of XBRL for any company filing electronically. For multinationals, XBRL is a huge money- and time-saver as it lets companies file in all countries using the same process.

Holland, New Zealand, and Australia are already accepting tax returns and other government-required documents in XBRL. Over 90 percent of Spanish banks now report in XBRL. Both England and India have reporting programs for *private* companies. XBRL is going to help build a worldwide semantic web of financial information, just in time to meet the needs of a growing international economy.

The Product Manager

"We realized XBRL was going to be big," says Mark Bolgiano, who was hired in 2006 to be the first CEO of XBRL US. "We just didn't realize *how* big, and how important a role it would play in rebuilding our financial system years later. But we knew that if every public company in the United States was going to use XBRL to file reports, it would have to be professionalized."

Bolgiano took a team of enthusiastic volunteers and gave many of them jobs. XBRL US was a consortium of companies, regulators, accounting firms, and software companies. Under Bolgiano's guidance, they built a framework for reporting using U.S. generally acceptable accounting practices (US GAAP). Bolgiano explains, "It took the better part of a year and about two hundred different contributors, but we've now laid a solid foundation for XBRL to grow." Bolgiano's team delivered the **US GAAP taxonomy**, a structured dictionary of over 12,000 terms defined precisely, according to the exact specifications of the SEC and other government and accounting bodies.

Bolgiano's public-private partnership also hammered out a taxonomy for mutual funds (about 2,000 terms) and plans to build many more, according to a master plan shared with XBRL International. The team builds tools, tests, preparers' guides, and a rollout and maintenance plan for all the new standards that will be built on top of the taxonomy backbone.*

The taxonomy encapsulates the rules from many different domains of expertise, and reporting software can read and understand those rules. Now you can't file an invalid report because the software won't allow it. As the taxonomy is updated, everyone's software updates simultaneously.

Bolgiano says XBRL arrived just in time: "We are providing tools to resolve the financial crisis, which is really a crisis of information. I hope it will play an important role in the Obama administration's disclosure and transparency effort. There's a lot left to do, but it's remarkable how far we've come in just the past few years."

XBRL is already participating in the TARP program. In 2009, the Obama administration mandated XBRL reports for all companies with over $5 billion in sales. Ultimately, all U.S. public companies will file reports in XBRL. This involves a one-time cost for companies to make sure their systems and data conform to the standard, but as XBRL grows in acceptance, the tools and processes get cheaper and the reports get more accurate.

The benefits to shareholders are tremendous. Soon, all the XBRL filings will be online in a new database that will replace EDGAR with a semantic

---

* I encourage you to explore the taxonomy at **viewer.xbrl.us.**

feed of corporate reports. Using the new XBRL resource, regulators will have a dashboard that shows all reports as soon as they come in, and the software can flag any irregularities immediately. XBRL and the semantic web of reporting data will be Chairman Cox's lasting legacy.

Case Study: United Technologies

In 2005, United Technologies, the forty-third largest corporation in the United States, with over 200,000 employees, produced their quarterly and annual business reports using Microsoft Word, fed by various spreadsheets. The total processing time for a 10-Q quarterly report for the SEC was 845 hours. After minimal training and a small investment in new software, United Technologies' staff was producing 10-Q reports in XBRL in under 700 hours. They now prepare, proofread, and transmit reports directly to EDGAR using XBRL, without going through Word.

As John Stantial, director of financial reporting for United Technologies, writes in his report online:

> The benefits to XBRL come in the future when tagged information is readily available from all companies and can be accessed electronically for analysis, benchmarking, reporting uses and financial modeling. Not only can XBRL enhance external financial reporting, but it can also be applied internally for cost accounting, performance measurement, analysis and decision-making purposes.[13]

Case Study: FDIC Call Report

The FDIC call report is a quarterly filing from more than 8,000 federally insured banks, showing their closing balance sheets and a number of risk parameters. Originally, they were mailed in on standard paper forms. Then they were faxed. The FDIC had to check for logic or math errors and look for discrepancies that needed more explanation. In 2004, it took banks forty-five days after the end of each quarter to compile a call report, have it verified, and submit it. The FDIC returned more than a third of the reports, asking for more information.

On October 1, 2005, the FDIC began requiring all submitting banks to use an XBRL format tailored to build a call report. But it did more. It sent the banks the full taxonomy (terms, definitions, and business rules) so the banks could do their own error checking. The rules caught all the logic and math errors, so banks couldn't send in a faulty report. They also caught anything out of range (like a significant change from the previous quarter), so the banks could include explanations and footnotes in the first draft.

This entire system cost the FDIC $40 million to implement. All 8,200 financial institutions adopted it immediately. Compliance was 100 percent. Logic and math errors were reduced by 100 percent. That's right – 100 percent. (The only errors the system didn't catch were those extreme cases the business rules weren't designed to handle.) Today, banks send their call reports in within fifteen days, and some manage to file call reports within twenty-four hours of the quarter's end.

The common call report makes the FDIC much more agile, and it enables new policy changes. For example, the FDIC charges all banks the same insurance premium, regardless of risk. Now, with new data, the FDIC could charge each bank a premium according to its risk profile. Eventually, the FDIC could eliminate the requirement for quarterly reports entirely, going to continuous reporting that is simply a by-product of doing business. Does that sound familiar?

The savings to banks and the FDIC are enormous. The FDIC gets an accurate picture of their lenders thirty days earlier than before. How much was that worth in the fall of 2008? It's impossible to say exactly, but it seems the FDIC's $40 million investment has paid off many times over. Imagine how much paper forms *still* cost the banking industry – and yours!

The Power Shift

As Mark Bolgiano puts it, "We're on the steep part of the curve now, which puts us pretty far ahead of most other information-based industries. Our next big challenge is to work with the international financial reporting standards community to integrate all the XBRLs around the world." Because XBRL has so much momentum, the power shift in financial reporting is just ahead. Once we have reports online in a format all software can understand, the semantic ecosystem will start to take shape. Here is a sample of projects already started or in the works:

General ledger (XBRLGL): These open-data formats will bridge the gap between transactions and the financial report. Just by doing business your books are done and your reports are filed.

Canonical business languages: These provide open formats for all the transaction-based forms businesses use in the front office every day. The Universal Business Language (UBL) from Open Applications Group (OAGI) provides standard forms for invoices, shipping forms, receipts, sales ledgers, expense reports, and many other forms in daily use.

Rating bonds: XBRL paves the way for future systems that will allow debt instruments to be rated in real time, as loans are made, in context with other such debt and the overall macroeconomic conditions, using the results of actual sales in the marketplace daily. Imagine a bond rating adjusted every night at midnight by software, rather than having an analyst do it under a conflict of interest the day before the company files for bankruptcy.

Research: The research information markup language (RIXML) is a global standard for releasing investment research reports. When research reports come out onto the open web, they will be easy to compare and incorporate directly into other reports.

Alerts: If a material event happens – the CEO goes in for emergency surgery, a freeze damages the crops, a strike prevents a shipment, a hostile takeover offer comes in – the company must announce it. When something important happens, the company can report it in near real time, rather than waiting and confusing investors.

Variances: Alerts go both ways. Once all the transactions and assets are described online, watchdogs will scan the open web for any discrepancies or situations that are out of their normal range.

Derivatives: An existing language called Financial Products Markup Language, or FPML, describes derivative financial products and business processes that allow buyers to create a more uniform, reliable market.

Interactive maps: Imagine being able to see all the corporate debt of the entire world in an interactive fashion that would allow you to slice it by region, risk level, pricing, asset value, delinquency, collateralization, or structured product. This would be like looking at a weather map of the data, with the ability to slice and dice the information however you want.

Real-time accounting: When companies switch from patching their ERP systems to using a transaction-recording backbone that is central to all systems, they will be able to close their books every day.

Integration: Fujitsu, which has almost 400 subsidiaries and over 150 systems connected to its accounting system, turned to XBRL GL as an information backbone that ties all the systems together with a royalty-free, vendor-neutral format. The common format lets Fujitsu add more systems and acquire new companies without trying to get all systems to speak one another's languages.

Analytics: With all the information online, it's much easier to make direct comparisons. Since the information doesn't move, analysts can employ many fewer people to wrangle data. They can now focus on interpretation rather than gathering information.

Government integration: The governments of Japan, Holland, Australia, and New Zealand already receive XBRL files for tax, compliance, and other requirements. Holland and Australia now allow submissions to more than forty different government agencies using a single file. Australia has saved companies more than $A800 million per year in preparing data for the government.

Xʙʀʟ Mash-Ups

*To see **XBRL** simply as a means of marking up financial statements at the end of a financial reporting period is to miss the rest of the iceberg. If financial items are automatically tagged upon their creation using a system like **SAP**, the rich analysis can be filtered through the enterprise and to suppliers. Triggers and reports can be generated on the fly. Knowledge workers will be manipulating **XBRL** without knowing it by its accurate, albeit consonant-heavy, name.*

– Derek Abdinor

What's Next

Xʙʀʟ is an important step in the right direction, but it doesn't give us the full transparency we need to protect investors. It's far too easy to hide problematic, significant, even illegal details by sweeping them into various components of a report. In Chapter 14, we'll see examples of large, well-known companies hiding illegal practices in their annual reports with ease. The next step will involve more transparency at a lower level, possibly at the transaction level. We don't need more rules and regulations; we need more transparency to give investors the power to pull information and prevent companies from hiding it. Whatever ultimately helps reform the markets will be built on top of xʙʀʟ.

I hope people in your company are already thinking about how to leverage XBRL to the fullest. The next step would be to join some of these organizations and help them expand their standards. The coming semantic web of interconnected financial reporting data is already well under way – be sure you're actively participating to get the most out of it.

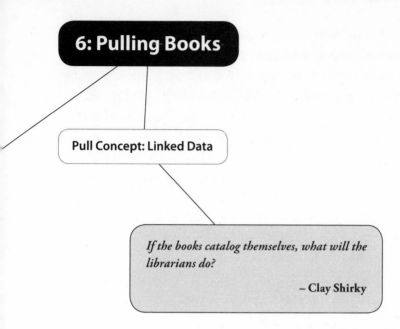

6: Pulling Books

Pull Concept: Linked Data

If the books catalog themselves, what will the librarians do?

– Clay Shirky

IN APRIL 2009, ON EASTER SUNDAY, the gay, lesbian, bisexual, and transgender communities were up in arms. Without warning, some of Amazon's 57,000 books on gay and lesbian topics were invisible to searches and lost their sales rankings, while *Playboy* and other titles were still showing up. Gay and lesbian authors saw their sales figures go to zero. Why had they been singled out on Easter? A message? A change in policy? Thousands of people sent Twitter messages using the keyword **#Amazonfail**, encouraging cancellation of orders, a widespread boycott, and sale of the company's stock the next morning.

All this because of a programming glitch that was fixed a few hours later. As it turned out, an employee in France had mistakenly made a change to a database, inadvertently flipping the "adult" field from FALSE to TRUE, immediately disenfranchising entire categories of books. Amazon employees went on red alert and spent their Easter Sunday tracking down the problem. By Monday morning, the system was back to normal, but the damage to the company's reputation had already been done. A misunderstanding about metadata had caused thousands of people to turn against a company they had previously trusted.

There is a lot of information in books, and there is also a rapidly growing universe of information *about* books. It's changing the way we write, purchase, and use books. As Amazon.com knows, it also plays a role in the relationship between retailers and shoppers. This chapter tells the story of how we pull books through the supply chain to different kinds of consumers using different kinds of metadata.*

The Book Industry Consortium

In North America, there are roughly 4 million books in print. Every year, publishers bring about 300,000 new English-language books to market, and there are 30 to 40 *million* changes made to the metadata. There are thousands of publishers, but the top 200 account for the vast majority of titles sold. This is a $40 billion industry (wholesale) in the United States, and still growing. The people in this business cooperate willingly because they've seen how much better their lives are since they agreed to use the ONline Information eXchange format (ONIX). In the United States, the consortium in charge of ONIX is a nonprofit, the Book Industry Study Group. With a budget of less than $1 million from contributing companies, BISG now has more than 250 members using ONIX, with more converting all the time. They meet at the two big book fairs every year, where committees actively work on standards for the next release.

All software vendors now build their software around ONIX, which carries no royalty. Publishers and distributors can have different styles of putting information into their ONIX files, but in general, once your book description is in ONIX, it is portable and reusable. For example,

---

* In this chapter I have made up names and companies to represent a composite picture of the many people I interviewed at different companies.

a publisher can include catalog copy, so when the spring catalog is printed, the publisher can send the book list in ONIX format to the printing software, which lays out the catalog automatically. The publisher uses the same file to send information through the supply chain and to communicate with publishers in other countries. Search engines see an ONIX file and know that it describes a book.

After the 2.0 release of ONIX, the distributors started a voluntary certification process for publishers providing ONIX feeds. To get certified, a publisher submits a file describing any number of books, and the distributors run it through their software and produce a score. At the moment, they just check that the thirty core fields have content in them and none is left blank. If all thirty fields for all books in a publisher's catalog are occupied, the publisher is certified.

ONIX has a classification system that includes about 3,000 subjects and categories. It has fifty-two top-level categories: for example, Computers, Art, History, Fiction, True Crime. And each section has one to three levels of subsections: for example, History / Africa / General. You might think that 3,000 subject headings are enough for a bookstore, but it's not even close, as we'll soon see.

More and more, a title is something that can be published in several different ways. Some novels have been distributed one chapter at a time. Some novels in Japan are now available only on mobile phones, as they are written. The BISG tries to keep ahead of these developments and has several active committees in all areas of technology. For a group of people rooted in a paper-based world, they are far ahead of their counterparts in most other industries.

Very few industries are on version 3.0 of a major open-data format. The industry's first goal has been to reduce errors and thereby reduce costs. A chart of corrections made to book data would show a strong gradual decline since the adoption of ONIX. The next goal is to continue to streamline the pathways of book metadata and reduce the number of hands that touch it on the way.

The Publisher

Tom is a publisher with 150,000 titles in his catalog. From all divisions, the company brings out 3,000 new books every year. He joined the BISG in 2000 and now sits on several committees, including Identity and eBooks.

In the old days, Tom's company produced what was called "the file." The file was in Excel, and it went to a dozen distributors. The company committed to ONIX in 2000, partly because of Tom's involvement. It took less than a year to build a new catalog system so everyone in the company could write book descriptions using the new software and they would be exported as complete and valid ONIX. The catalog has ONIX descriptions for all books the company has in print for the last 180 days and all those that will come out in the next 180 days.

All titles published since 2000 are now up to date. He still has about 120,000 titles in pre-ONIX format that are very incomplete and inconsistent. It's his back list, most of which is out of print, and while he'd like to update this information, he doesn't have the resources to do it. Maybe he'll get to it someday, but a complete ONIX catalog isn't on his top-ten list of things to do. As his CEO says, "Data is a black hole. I can pour all the money in the world in there, and I'm not sure what's going to come out." So Tom goes carefully, building support for data cleansing and staying on top of new developments in the BISG.

Tom's major day-to-day hassle is getting the metadata right at the source. Some books are in the wrong categories. Some have misspellings. Switching to ONIX let him move three people who used to do data format translation to a new department that does data cleansing.

Despite his significant investment in ONIX-formatted metadata, his distributors start making changes as soon as they receive the file, just as they had done previously with the old Excel spreadsheets. Distributors often make changes to author and title fields, hoping bookstores will prefer their version. He would love to send his data straight to the retailers, but the retailers want a handful of sources, not thousands.

On Sundays, Tom's system automatically puts the latest file on a secure server, and all the distributors can get it automatically whenever they want. He uploads a delta (update) file on Wednesdays and Fridays. Overall, Tom's ONIX catalog is much more accurate and complete than it was before. It sells more books. Because of ONIX, the supply chain is fairly efficient. Everyone can make a change to the metadata on Wednesday and see it reflected on the Barnes and Noble web site by Monday (Amazon takes much longer). Ideally, it would change in seconds.

The Small Publisher

Mary's company publishes architecture books; she brings out about 20 titles a year and it has 350 books in its catalog. Of those, only 120 are still in print. Mary has survived industry consolidation by keeping her headcount down, printing offshore, and publishing a series of up-to-the-minute e-books on current trends that have been well received. She runs a profitable business and has an interest in keeping her metadata visible and findable online.

Mary knows the value of ONIX and has no interest in dragging her feet, but she can't afford to have a staff of programmers. Instead, she uses online software that lets her build her catalog from anywhere. She has a part-time employee who works from home making sure the data is complete and accurate. She can start a new project right in the browser window and keep adding to the book's description until she wants to release it to her catalog.

The software builds and maintains an e-commerce web site, where buyers can log in and see wholesale prices. The software also lets Mary offer a complete store on her web site and take orders directly from consumers. She gets a trickle of orders from consumers this way, and while many publishers aren't interested in direct selling, she doesn't mind selling directly if she can get the full retail price for a book. She enjoys the margins and is happy to pack and ship. She has also gotten into promoting her site online and buying traffic. The software service pays for itself in the first week of every month.

The Distributor

Of the 4 million books in print in North America, about a quarter now have ONIX descriptions to some degree. Almost all of the 300,000 English-language titles U.S. publishers bring out every year are now in ONIX. There are only four major book distributors, and they do a lot of the same things. I'll blend them all into one fictional person named Paul.

Paul's company sells books from over 20,000 publishers, ranging from huge to single authors. The vast majority of the publishers are very small businesses that still send in their book descriptions on spreadsheets and require conversion to ONIX. Today, 98 percent of the new titles in his catalog are in ONIX format.

Like other distributors, Paul charges a subscription fee for his metadata catalog of about 800,000 titles. The company adds value by making sure the data is appropriate for various clients. For example, it makes changes to book descriptions for libraries that it doesn't make for bookstores. When it finds a true mistake, the company sends an email back to the publisher so the publisher can correct it once and for all. But most of his "corrections" simply differentiate the company's catalog from those of the other distributors. For example, there are specific "zones" for kids, starting at age five, so the company has to change "for ages eight and up" to "for ages eight to eleven."

ONIX is the structure – the container – and it's fixed by agreement. But there's little agreement on exactly how all the fields should be used.

Because Paul's company aggregates hundreds of feeds, and because all publishers use slightly different internal standards, he needs to keep about twenty people on staff just to massage publishers' ONIX files and incorporate the non-ONIX files into a consolidated catalog. For example, if a title is in a series, publishers often put the series number in the title field; this needs to be fixed because ONIX has a separate field for the series number. Even though it's a lot of work, his correction staff is down from fifty just five years ago. The company's metadata standards have been around since the old paper days; the unit is profitable and is seen as a competitive advantage inside the company.

The Retailer

Retail Books, Inc.,* an online retailer, wants to sell as many books as possible. The mantra in this company is: "More metadata sells more books." This company counts a full 35 percent of sales driven by recommendations, professional reviews, and customer reviews. Like most other large retailers, Retail Books buys all the ONIX feeds from all the distributors. On its site and for its audience, a consistent experience is important, so it uses a proprietary scheme to mix and match titles, author names, and book descriptions. Its metadata looks different from its competitors', and Retail Books likes it that way.

Retail Books has a team of people who scan book covers, tables of contents, and the first chapters of many books. They add book reviews from trusted sources and customers. The company has its own special non-ONIX format, which it makes available through an Application Programming Interface (API), a set of standards that makes it possible for another site to download Retail's catalog data. Plenty of other sites,

---

* Retail Books, Inc. is a fictional company, used here for example purposes. This section is based on Amazon.com, but I did not interview anyone there. Any errors or omissions are mine.

both commercial and noncommercial, thrive on these feeds, so non-ONIX book descriptions are all over the web.

What happened to the ONIX? Publishers send out ONIX feeds, distributors change the descriptions into different flavors of ONIX, retailers buy all the different feeds, and use whichever versions they want for their web site, recombining them to try to outdo each other. Then this retailer strips away the ONIX container for its own system and feeds the resulting mix to hundreds of other sites around the web! As someone once said, the great thing about standards is that we have so many to choose from.

The Standards Setter

One company that has a unique role in U.S. book publishing is Bowker, which has been distributing book metadata since 1872. Bowker is the U.S. agent in charge of assigning a unique International Standard Book Number (ISBN) to every physical book. For example, the novel *Moby-Dick* comes in dozens of versions and has as many ISBN numbers. Since each ISBN has its own ONIX file, often from different publishers, it's impossible to have standardized information that's common to all those files. Furthermore, other publishers produce foreign editions, causing further **semantic dispersion** of the data around a single title. All the worldwide metadata for the Harry Potter series alone would fill a book thicker than this one.

About 250,000 e-books now have ISBNs, although audio books and books delivered as electronic files don't have ISBNs. Print-on-demand books and book chapters published on their own don't have unique numbers, either. Bowker is working on an extension system to handle future ways books will be delivered.

Bowker has its own subject classification scheme, which differs from that of ONIX. It has 80,000 subjects and categories. Most large publishers and all the online bookstores buy Bowker's classification scheme. Its approach is to add value to publisher's data and then sell it back to them (and anyone else who will buy it).

The Prosumer

If the open semantic web of book metadata refuses to get going formally, a few people will start building it themselves. We'll peek over the reading lamp of Zoe, a fictional reader who represents many people in the book-reading community.

Zoe reads books. A lot of books. She blogs about books and keeps a list of every book she has ever read. She's a member of Readers Anonymous, an online community of reading addicts. She keeps a list of books she is willing to loan at neighBORROW.com, a lending site. But she spends most of her time at a few big web sites I'll talk about in more depth here. Although there are literally hundreds of sites where you can enter your book list, the top three together account for over 2 million visitors per month.[14]

Goodreads.com is a free, ad-supported, venture-backed web site where you can build your book lists, write reviews, tweet what you just read to your followers on Twitter, see what your friends are reading, and share with others in the community. The basic metadata comes from Amazon Web Services via its APIs. The site claims more than 1.5 million registered users who have rated over 30 million books. Users add reviews, build their own categories, and share their lists with others. Over 2,400 dedicated volunteer librarians chase down metadata requests from the community and help keep things up to date.

A similar site is **LibraryThing.com**, with over 600,000 members and 36 million books cataloged. Members have added more than 46 million tags to book descriptions and contributed over 1.3 million cover scans and 31,000 author photos! The site makes money – people enter 200 books for free, and if they want to build a larger inventory they pay either $10 per year or $25 for life. Once again, none of the stock metadata is in ONIX format – it comes from Amazon and from almost 700 library feeds in MARC format (see next section). Perhaps the most interesting statistic is that the LibraryThing community disambiguates over 2,000 titles every *day*, finding duplicates, misspellings, etc.

The **Open Library** project, started by Internet Archive founder Brewster Kahle, wants to be the Wikipedia of structured book metadata. The goal of the site is one web page for every book ever published. So far, they have gathered information on over 20 million books and have scanned the full text of over 1 million books, which you can read on the site. It's a mostly volunteer project, with a small paid staff, and everything is open and free. Zoe spends time here adding descriptive information to the book pages that already exist and looking for errors. She dedicates her Thursday nights to helping the Open Library community however she can.

Book Metadata

The only person who can categorize everything is everybody.

– Clay Shirky

Zoe feels good helping the community of book lovers add information about books that anyone can use. She believes book metadata should come out of the deep online silos into the open amateur realm, where more people can use it. Another reason Zoe belongs to and is active in these sites is for the social value, which shouldn't be underestimated. She meets and makes friends on these sites.

The Librarian

In 1876, Melvil Dewey founded a company called the Library Bureau, which made index cards and cabinets for libraries. Dewey set the standard for the index card at 75 x 125 millimeters (3 x 5 inches), with a single hole at the bottom. Soon after, the Library of Congress got into the game, selling sets of cards describing books to libraries, who preferred to purchase them rather than make their own. In the 1960s, the Library of Congress created an electronic standard, MAchine-Readable Cataloging (MARC), which put book descriptions into electronic files so they could be printed on 3 x 5 cards. In the 1970s, libraries could dial into a proprietary system, select their books, add their own data, and send the resulting file to the print shop. Months later, they would receive a custom-built set of cards that fit nicely into their wooden cases.

Today, library metadata is big business. With over 70,000 member libraries in 112 countries, the Online Computer Library Center (OCLC) is the world's largest consortium. It publishes WorldCat, an electronic "union catalog" of more than 130 million publication descriptions drawn from over 1 billion holdings. Most libraries pay a membership fee to access WorldCat's database, earning OCLC revenues of $85 million per year.[15]

The WorldCat metadata format is MARC, developed and updated by the Library of Congress. MARC, now in its twenty-first version, has become a patchwork quilt of tags and fields that try to be all things to all libraries in all languages. It still essentially describes how to print a 3 x 5 card, with plenty of extra features thrown in for computer-based searching.* WorldCat has the information everyone wants online. But the OCLC is doing its best to retain control and hold onto its shrinking revenues.

---

* By the mid-1990s, most U.S. libraries had abandoned 3 x 5 cards.

The Library of Congress has a different vision. It employs more than 500 catalogers adding metadata to over 300,000 new titles per year. The library maintains more than 14 million descriptions of software titles, rare books, plays, photographs, posters, manuscripts, magazines, maps, music, microfiche, and more. The Library of Congress is getting ready to put all its catalog resources online as linked data and help other libraries do the same.

In this world, it's everyone against the OCLC, and everyone is winning. Volunteers and professionals are working to reassemble book descriptions, making WorldCat irrelevant. Here are the upcoming stars who are laying the foundation that will take library metadata into the twenty-first century:

National Science Digital Library (metadataregistry.org): This organization was initially funded by the National Science Foundation to build a hub for all the many vocabularies, classes, terms, and other resources scientists will need. It lets people (and programs) call these resources by name, find them, and incorporate them into any search or system. The registry doesn't build taxonomies, but it helps you link the taxonomies you need into your system and keep it up to date. This key piece of plumbing is already working, helping people build vocabularies properly and flexibly, and is available to all online. (As Diane Hillmann, one of the visionaries behind the registry, says: "This is not your grandmother's metadata.")

Resource Description and Access (RDA): The rules for cataloging are complex and important. If people use different rules, the data will be inconsistent. Until now, the Anglo-American cataloging rules have been written in a standard reference book, similar to the *Chicago Manual of Style*. The national libraries of Britain, Canada, Australia, and the United States are encoding the rules in semantic formats that can plug into future software, so any catalog or data file will automatically conform to the rules.

Library of Congress Subject Headings (LCSH): The LCSH taxonomy has over 280,000 subject categories – far richer than anything used by publishers or even Amazon.com. In contrast to the ONIX headings, the LCSH taxonomy has subcategories like:

> *Massachusetts – History – Colonial period, ca. 1660–1775 – Juvenile literature*

Each term has broader terms above, narrower terms below, and similar terms from other vocabularies. For most of its life, librarians at the Library of Congress have kept it under strict control. Now it's online in a semantic format called an ontology (see Chapter 12) and anyone can take it, modify it, and use it in any way he likes. You can see it at **id.loc.gov.** This is a true piece of semantic web infrastructure already working, bringing 100 years of cataloging experience to the open web.

Virtual International Authority File (VIAF.org): The VIAF, organized by the Library of Congress, will be a directory pointing to dozens of national library files describing names of people, places, companies, and things in many languages. This semantic hub is being set up as an online service to hand out name information to any computer that asks for it. For example, if a person in Tokyo searches for information about this book, she might find a Google listing describing the book, and my name will be pulled out of VIAF.org and rendered in Japanese characters in real time, because the National Library of Japan has provided my name in its feed to VIAF.org. *That's* pulling metadata!

Library of Congress on Flickr: The Library of Congress is really getting into the semantic web. In 2008, it put up about

6,000 photos from its collection, asking *ordinary people* to help tag them with keywords and identifiers to make them more searchable. Search for "Library of Congress" on Flickr, and if you recognize people or places or anything else in a photo, you can help the LC build a better catalog!

Linked Data (Linkeddata.org): This is a central starting point for linked data of all kinds, started by Sir Tim Berners Lee and others. The resources needed for books will overlap with the resources needed for knowledge. There will be thousands of online dictionaries, thesauri, taxonomies, and ontologies describing all the niche areas of interest. You'll find many of the resources I mention in this book linked from this central directory.

Since the first library, which was probably built around 1900 B.C. in present-day Iraq, libraries have all been built on the same model: Acquire copies of works and help people find them and use them. But if most people are just trying to get their questions answered, how does the library of today help them do that?

The library of the future will be online. It will be a collection of specialized content, search engines, and starting points that can help you get answers to questions, find things you're looking for, and find things you didn't know you were looking for. If it's a physical object, the library of the future will link to the most definitive reference page describing that object, or to several reference pages about that object, and a list of locations where you can find it. Eventually, most books and photos will be scanned and their contents made findable online. You'll get the answers to your questions right from your kitchen or your phone.

Small branch libraries are the libraries of the future. They will provide a good place to sit quietly and research online, a place for kids to learn, and meeting spaces for learning-related events. They will have minimal staff and probably won't be open all day. There may not be very many; schools will do just as well. Our monstrous downtown libraries with their stacks of books and huge staffs won't make it to the middle of the century.

The Search Engine

"Who cares about a standard format?" says Frances Haugen, who works at the Google Books project. "Just put it out there on the web where we can crawl it. The web is messy – we can reconcile the different versions of a record into something useful." Google wants to compile the world's largest card catalog, collecting information on every book ever written. This information will help make books more discoverable and help users search the contents of books as well.

Search engines don't need a single web site where all the book's metadata resides. They can pull structured data from all over the web and serve it to people looking for information as they need it. Google already aggregates more than a hundred different metadata sources in dozens of languages. Its programs deal with data inconsistency every day. Publishers, after all, are as bad as distributors – few companies take the time to develop consistent internal standards that comply with industry norms.

"Think of all the book enthusiasts out there," Haugen continues. "I think all the books in the United States could be cataloged in five years using volunteers. We just need to give people the tools to do it – like open-source cataloging software and bar-code-reading programs for mobile phone cameras. These records could open up new possibilities for interacting with books because people would be free to do anything with the metadata. If you're looking for a particular book, you may want to know which copy is nearest you. It might be your neighbor on the other side of the wall.

"I'm a big fan of mashing up metadata," she explains (my fingers typing in Dvorak as fast as she talks). "Suppose you're looking for a particular book published in the 1950s – how would you know it even exists and what it contains? What about building knowledge models out of book content in a certain domain? Then you could be searching for chapters, concepts, quotes, formulas, facts, and figures. People could ask questions and the books could answer collectively. Only volunteers have the time to put all this information online."

Should there be a central repository? "There's no center of book meta-data. We don't even need a full name space. The web is messy. Google has designed fault-tolerant ways to interpret it. A single consistent system just won't scale. Expecting and encouraging diversity does scale. Anything hierarchical will break sooner than later.

"Imagine the world five years from now. Millions of books have been scanned. For the first time, this content is truly accessible to users all around the world. What if there are new ways to monetize all that content for their rights holders? The Audubon Society could provide an incredibly high quality library for their members; through their curation, we can learn how best to present all that is known about birds. The cycle is virtuous – the more human signals (tags, reviews, etc.), the better the search becomes, the more books users will find, the more signals we get, and so on.

"The filter is the future. There should be a million different curators, and you should find the filters that work for you. You'll choose by how people blog about, tag, tweet, rate, or annotate the books they are excited about. In a world where a thousand different publishing houses have the same chance of producing the next Harry Potter, you will no longer rely on the well-known name brands. You need to ask questions, filter, forage, find. Twitter may soon be a more important way to learn about books than the *New York Times Book Review*."

The Book of the Future

The dematerialization of books has been in progress for a decade already, and printed books have supposedly been at death's door ever since. Now, however, I believe we are finally at the beginning of the end. According to blogger Mark Coker, e-books' $114 million in sales to end users in 2008 represents 0.5 percent of the trade book market, and he expects e-book sales to top 6 percent by 2013. That's not bad for publishers, who are busy bringing their back list to life in e-book format, but it is bad for paper makers.

Soon, e-books will be mainstream, and that will bring big changes. An e-book on your next-generation reader is sitting right next to the rest of the entire web. It looks like a long column of text, without page numbers. The idea of pages will start to disappear and be replaced by semantic markers – tags that specify what the writing is about. Readers will annotate and start discussions around the topics in books, making e-book reading a social activity. As you read, you'll see what others have said about the writing, even watch a video or listen to a recording. You may find yourself foraging off in a new direction, leaving the book behind. The author herself may guide you off toward new discoveries outside the book. Reading a popular diet book? You can subscribe to the comments of one or more researchers in the field to see which statements are backed up by evidence.

The world of blogs, books, and documents will mesh seamlessly in many different formats. In fact, you may not be reading this right now. You may be listening to my voice – or someone else's. Will my next book be a paper book? That depends on my readers. I'll have to follow their demands and give them my thoughts the way they want to pull them into their lives.

The Bookstore of the Future

I can tell you pretty accurately the future of retail bookselling. The bookstore of the future will be a small retail store. It will stock a few hundred popular books and a printing machine that can print every book ever written. If you want the heft and feel of a printed book, you'll print it right at the bookstore. When the metadata and the data come together, when the price of the technology comes down, many coffee houses could have a machine that prints any book ever written. Then people like Zoe will stop by every day for a double daily dose.

It will probably be at least twenty years until the sales of e-books overtakes sales of our sixteenth-century friend, the printed book. The twenty-first century will, for the most part, be the end of the line for physical libraries and bookstores, a shift that will be good for writers and readers, put perhaps not for publishers and distributors. Today's e-book readers and computers will give way to the always-connected screens of tomorrow. As we will learn in Chapter 7, the bookstore of the future will likely be . . . no bookstore at all.

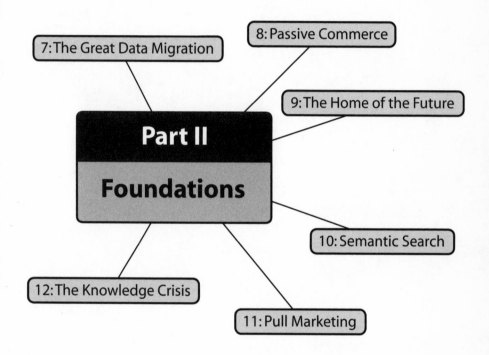

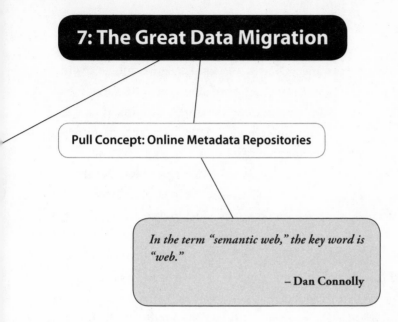

7: The Great Data Migration

Pull Concept: Online Metadata Repositories

In the term "semantic web," the key word is "web."

— Dan Connolly

LOOK DOWN ON ANY LARGE CITY FROM ABOVE on a weekday and you'll see people walking from building to building; cars, taxis, and buses moving people on the roads; trains gliding on tracks; boats arriving at the docks. You'll see big trucks coming in from the highways, their payloads broken down and brought into the city on small trucks. That's very similar to the way information moves today.

And that's the problem we're going to fix in this chapter. Not only do we spend far too much time chasing down information in far-flung places, but it has no chance to keep up to the minute if we're always moving it. Once again, we've gotten good at imitating our old-fashioned ways of sending notes, letters, packages, and catalogs, and it hasn't scaled well at all. How many times have you left a document on a computer you don't have, or you've emailed an attachment to someone and then made changes and had to re-email it again, or two people have edited a document in different places, and now it's split and needs to be recombined? Why is it we always know where our applications are, but we often can't find the data? Which is harder to replace?

It's time we learned to stream and syndicate. The main message of this chapter is that on the semantic web, **data never moves** – it stays in one place where we can always find it, use it, pull it, and combine it with other information. We've already seen two important online resources: the SEC's centralized XBRL resource and the distributed linked data of the book world, which is rapidly coming together to make the information in books findable, even though it's not in a central database.

In this chapter, I introduce the concept of **universal descriptor databases** for products, services, and companies: one place where you can find definitive information on any product ever made or any service anyone provides. In some cases, there will be single databases that hold all the necessary descriptions. In others, the information will be linked and distributed. It doesn't matter. The semantic web is about available, up-to-date metadata that can always be found.

I'll also introduce the concept of the **online birth certificate** for every product and many services. These two resources will be an important part of the infrastructure that will let us pull information through much faster than we can today. I'll end with a description of our media, hardware, and software. See if you can get ahead of me and predict what I'm going to say.

Sales Tax

First, an example of syndication and eliminating the middleman. Sales tax is metadata. In the United States, 45,000 cities charge sales tax, with 9,000 agencies responsible for setting tax rates. Because all point-of-purchase software must calculate sales tax when necessary, a cottage industry of data aggregators has sprung up to meet the demand for calculating sales tax and printing out those charts you see taped near the cash register. Aggregators provide up-to-date tables and collect thousands of dollars per year in subscription fees. Software companies must regularly plug the new rates into their systems. If you need the most up-to-date information, you'll pay thousands of dollars each year in tax data subscriptions.

In the pull era, we'll do it differently. There will be a single name space and format for declaring sales tax rates, so the sales tax data lives online at all times. The federal server links to the servers in the tax jurisdictions, which are responsible for their own data. Now, your software doesn't need the tax tables or the middleman. It just takes the right number from its source each time. If a county or city changes a tax rate, the change ripples immediately through all systems, because no one copies it.*

Central Metadata Repositories

Now that we've done it for sales tax, why not do it with every piece of metadata we use every day? The **online product atlas** is where we'll find the definitive description of any product we're looking for.

As I write this, I'm shopping for a printer. At CNET.com, I can compare printers by height and weight. That's because they do such a good job gathering data (they actually weigh the products themselves). Looking at one printer on Amazon.com, I see that the weight of the product is 89 pounds and the shipping weight is 87 pounds! I see a page for an Olympus zoom lens with a picture of a Sony mouse! A pair of slippers is labeled "cashmere," but one owner says they're only 7 percent cashmere. For many products, the Wikipedia documentation is far superior to Amazon.com's or even the manufacturer's published information. There are product descriptions everywhere online, yet no single site or service has the staff to pull it all together and get it right.

---

* In reality, most software systems will maintain a local copy but will check each morning and update the number if there are any changes.

The product atlas contains a **master description** of each product. It is all things to all people, because you can filter to your heart's content and just see what you want to see. Each product has a description, with specifications, marketing copy, catalog data, photos, videos, manuals, installation instructions, updates, reviews, responses to issues, etc. I won't say each product has its own "page," because that's old-school thinking. In reality, the atlas is a complicated, flexible database. Catalogs can subscribe to the source information and present it in any way the buyer likes.

The atlas describes a production model and its various options. The description of a 2010 Mercedes 500SL will have thousands of pieces of information, lists of all the options (by the manufacturer) and compatibilities (with after-market products), and will have hundreds of photos, reviews, testimonials, and dozens of videos. The photos and reviews are of particular examples, but they are meant to represent the **class**, rather than a particular object. Every piece of information, from the type of transmission fluid to the color of the interior, has a unique name, so it can take its place in the structured web of product descriptions.

The online product atlas is a semantic wiki – a community of product mavens collaborating to populate an ever-expanding database of standard product descriptors. In the same way that IMDB.com describes films using hundreds of accurate data fields filled out by volunteers, the product atlas will describe every product, new or old, making those descriptions available for all to use.

As an example, the **GoodRelations product ontology** describes over 1 million products, including prices, from various sources. Because it's an ontology (see Chapter 12), it can hold a tremendous amount of information and make logical connections and conclusions, find compatibilities or conflicts, and include other ontologies as they appear. GoodRelations is an academic project that is now starting to make its way into several e-commerce systems. It updates twice a week, so companies can enter all their descriptions and prices and the information will flow through to thousands of e-commerce systems within a few days. The goal is to have extremely deep information on millions of products, providing a resource that can be plugged into any e-commerce system without limitation.

Wil Shipley, a programmer with a penchant for detail and cool ideas, built an application called **Delicious Monster** that has won many awards. To use it, you put a product with a bar code in front of your Mac or video camera and let it scan the bar code. It fetches the product's photo and description from a database and loads a virtual shelf with your inventory. It started with books, CDs, DVDs, and video games. Since all the metadata comes from Amazon, the program now catalogs tools, electronics, gadgets, apparel, etc. Thousands of people pay $40 for this tool to help them organize their stuff. It's a validation of market demand for many of the concepts in this chapter. See it for yourself at **Delicious-Monster.com.**

Dara O'Rourke, a professor of environmental and labor policy at the University of California, Berkeley, was upset by companies that didn't disclose the true nature of their ingredients in their products. In many products, he found ingredients known to cause birth defects, cancer, or toxic waste. He started a company called **GoodGuide** that builds a web database and mobile-phone apps for disclosing information and rating products on an environmental scale. Just scan a product's bar code and learn the real story behind the marketing copy. This could prevent many large companies that import products from other countries from passing toxic products on to consumers. It's not just a single web destination; someday, the information will become part of the plumbing of the semantic web, working with other product metadata. Check your household cleaners, shampoo, and baby products with your iPhone today at **Goodguide.com.**

To get a sense of what an individual product descriptor might look like, spend some time at **DPReview.com.** This site is run by one of the most hard-core product mavens on the planet, Phil Askey. He collects and displays extremely detailed information about digital cameras, all in a consistent format of his own design. If Phil, and others like him, become domain experts contributing to a common set of product descriptions, then the experts will get the tools they want and everyone will benefit.

There will be service atlases as well. Already, we have nonsemantic sites like FindLaw.com and LendingTree.com. In the pull era, all law firms will describe themselves on their own web sites using standard formats, and a central repository will make them findable.

The wine industry didn't have a central repository, so a start-up called **Snooth** built it, but in a smart way. Snooth harnessed the energy of wine lovers. Its 600,000 visitors per month have entered over 2 million wine reviews and descriptions. More than 10,000 retailers from fifty countries upload inventory and pricing information *daily*. Snooth searches the web and brings back prices from retailers' sites. The site's volunteers have already consolidated more than 3 million duplicate wine names, disambiguating a mess of nicknames and misspellings. You can search for wine by price and postal code in twelve countries, then go to the reseller's site and buy. Snooth is so big, it expects to get its wine description format ratified by the industry as a standard. It could serve as a model for other product description atlases to come.

Linked Data in the Cloud

Is the product atlas a single web site or just a mesh network of interconnected descriptions online? It doesn't matter. Because once the naming scheme works, it will look the same no matter where the information lives. That's why we say, "The web is the database." It's important to understand this technical point. If everything is online in standard formats using a unique naming scheme, it doesn't matter where it is, and you don't need a web site to access it. You can use the entire web as a resource – a structured data store – and that's exactly what a database is. These days, most people refer to this as **linked data**. In the pull era, we don't need to go to many web sites and use the search facility at each one. We use search engines, and everything works at web scale. (You'll find a collection of linked data sets at **LinkedData.org**, a web site started by Tim Berners-Lee and others.)

The Deep Web

Today, less than 1 percent of what's online is on visible web pages. The rest is buried deep in proprietary databases. It helps to see the content of the Internet broken into three layers:

The public web we normally see when searching and browsing for information online: at least 21 billion pages indexed by search engines.[16] This is a tiny fraction of the information online – the rest is in databases that have no "pages" but simply respond to search requests.

The deep web includes large data repositories that require their own internal searches: BN.com, Facebook, SuperPages.com, Craigslist, Grainger, and so forth – about 6 trillion documents generally not seen by search engines.

The private web we can only get access to if we qualify: corporate intranets, private networks, subscription-based services, and so on – about 3 trillion "pages" also not seen by search engines.[17]

The deep web is *hundreds of times* larger than the web most search engines index today. Linked data will bring all that information to the surface and make it findable.

Many search engines are starting to query the deep web, trying to bring some of it to the surface. But that's a temporary approach that doesn't have the power of the open web. I use the term "open web" to refer to all the information coming online in semantic formats so it can be shared and used in many different ways. Data stays online, available to anyone who has permission to access it. This is what we call **cloud computing**. Already, data centers for cloud computing now consume more than 1 percent of the world's electricity.[18] As cloud computing grows, the resources will live online anywhere and they will be called by name to come do their job. What makes cloud computing different from traditional data centers is that once everything is online, we can combine data and programs from many sources, bring them together as necessary, and let them go back to the cloud when we're done. In cloud computing, the computing part is done by applications online, not on a handset or on a computer.*

Names Matter, Locations Don't

Let's go back to the tax-rate example. Now that all the tax rates are online, how does your software find the right one? You might think the location of a piece of sales tax data would live somewhere online in the kind of location we're used to seeing – something like:

http://www.taxrates.gov/salestax/colorado/durango

But in practice, this rigid, server-based scheme doesn't work. The people in Durango need access to a federal server, and the federal web team has to keep up with all the changes to all the passwords, permissions, tax values, etc. Tax tables like that would be permanently out of date. Instead, the federal server should just link to each tax jurisdiction, which keeps its own set of tax rates using a common format and a shared name space. This lets each tax jurisdiction add and subtract tax rates as they are needed, forming a dynamic mesh of tax rates. In this scheme, we don't care where the tax rates are. The software **asks for them by name**, not by location, and that's very different from the way things are done today.

---

* For a good example of this kind of online-application ecosystem, visit **SalesForce. com**.

The Internet Domain Name System (DNS) helped get the web started, but now it's part of the problem, not part of the solution. Domain names, like YouTube.com, are fine. You can put your server anywhere you like, and the domain name system will point to it. But that's where the fun stops and the pain starts. All those slashes you see after the names are physical locations on the server, and that leads to tremendous inflexibility. Have you seen this video:

youtube.com/watch?v=voAntzB7EwE

No? You really should. It's an incredibly funny piece of deep web. YouTube doesn't require a unique name for each video; the software simply assigns a unique number to each new video as it is submitted, and that number is associated with the video's title, description, and comments. It seems like the least bad approach, because so many videos have the same title. But it is, in fact, a terrible idea, because it forces people to send actual addresses around (like the one above), rather than a unique name. Will that video still be at that web address in ten years? I'll bet you a pair of semantic underwear it won't be. (My apologies if it's already gone by the time you read this.)

In cloud computing, once you have a unique name for something, the unique name points to its current location. You can move your data anywhere and just update the address associated with the name.

Unique Name	Current Location of the Actual Data
Amazing Colour-Changing Card Trick by Quirkology	youtube.com/watch?v=voAntzB7EwE

This is **the first level of abstraction of the semantic web:** separating the name of something from its location. Now it doesn't matter where the item is – it can be anywhere online. I've said the data never moves, and I'll say it again several more times, but I don't really mean it. What I mean is: it doesn't matter where the data lives, or if it moves, as long as it has a unique name that never changes and you can find that unique name and follow it to the information you're looking for.

And that's the **great data migration** – structured data comes out of the deep web and onto the open web, forming the foundation of the semantic web. You can call this the civil engineering of the web – it powers the shift from push to pull. We'll never get to real-time transaction data until all the deep-web information comes online and is accessible in milliseconds.

Science Commons

In a few years, we'll see this name-space power shift take place for science researchers. Thanks to the efforts of Lawrence Lessig and John Wilbanks, most of the world's information on neuroscience will soon be linked in a meaningful way online. Science Commons is a nonprofit whose mission is to link all scientific research together to help researchers find what they are looking for. They are starting with neuroscience; then they hope to move on to other areas.

The goal is simple: to provide a common naming and structural framework for scientific research, linking data across all domains. To do this, Science Commons is promoting data standards, establishing name spaces and vocabularies, and building tools scientists can use to build the science web semantically. The key, says Wilbanks, is to unify the name spaces, forming a **name backbone** that researchers can connect to. Wilbanks wants to disambiguate the names of genes, viruses, diseases, chemical compounds, proteins, people, concepts, and all the relevant scientific terms necessary to make the research findable. Wilbanks's message to drug companies is: "Let the community take care of the names, so you can use the power of the crowd to link things together. Then you can spend your time and money asking better questions and getting meaningful answers from the entire community." This approach replaces relational databases with flexible linked meshes of structured data that lives permanently online and can be combined in many different ways. Science Commons has assembled and interlinked over 100 neuroscience models to their name backbone, with many more on the way. (Learn more at **ScienceCommons.org.**)

The Online Art Atlas

Works of art are very different from products and companies because art is even harder to classify and each piece is unique. Yet the central repository for art descriptions already exists – sort of. It's based on a format called Categories for the Description of Works of Art (CDWA Lite), a Getty Museum project that provides a format for describing works of art online. All museums now have collection management systems, and they can all export data in this common format. CDWA Lite is just a data container – a set of nineteen fields that together describe a work of art at a basic level. Even though some museums now fill in over 200 fields for a given piece of art, the nineteen fields they export are the art equivalent of an ONIX book description.

Every week, most museums put their updated catalog data online in CDWA Lite format for anyone to pick up. One company that picks it all up is **ARTstor.org**, a nonprofit offshoot of the Andrew W. Mellon Foundation. ARTstor now provides a catalog of over 700,000 images and descriptions of unique works of art. ARTstor charges institutions for access to the database as a way to pay for the service. However, all those descriptions are online and they *are* free, so anyone who wants to can come pick them up and build a free wiki-style art atlas. (Google? A start-up? You, gentle reader?) It wouldn't have as many descriptions as ARTstor at first, but it would probably become very popular. Once it gets started, the art fanatics will help fill it in quickly.

Digital Birth Certificates

Back to products. Assume the product-description atlases are all built and the generic descriptions are on the open web. To describe a *specific* product, like your car, you start with the generic description from the atlas and add information about its color, vehicle ID number, manufacture date, options, driving history, miles, and condition of interior, exterior, wheels, and so on. If you describe all those things about your car semantically, you've got a **digital birth certificate**. Fortunately, you won't have to make one. Your car, and everything else you own, will come with its own digital birth certificate when you buy it.

In the world of pull, each manufacturer will use semantic metadata to manage its entire production line from start to finish, so digital birth certificates appear online as a by-product of the goods rolling out of the factory. The car company will set up and manage the birth certificates or outsource them to a trusted partner. The **nursery** is a central repository containing all the records for every car the company makes. The data stays online forever as part of the car's metadata ecosystem.

Each birth certificate includes the car's serial number, color, and options, and links to all the digital birth certificates for every significant part made by an outside contractor. Each part has its description inside the universal product atlas, and these parts have birth certificates hosted online by their manufacturers. There are fields for describing most services. In fact, as a service is performed, the repair shop updates the birth certificate automatically. So the car's birth certificate always reflects the condition of the actual car, and that can include every fill-up and every mile ever driven.

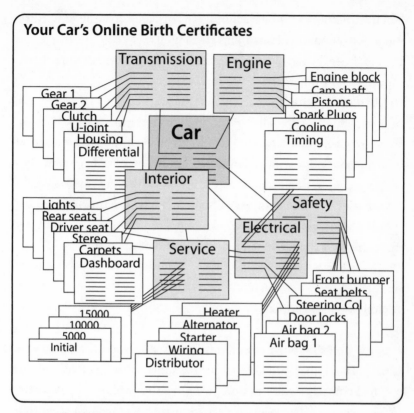

Your Car's Online Birth Certificates

Each car's information is hosted and maintained by the company that builds a product or provides a service. Many subcomponents have birth certificates that all link to the product's overall birth certificate.

The birth certificate stays current throughout a product's life. A camera's birth certificate will tell you how many photos the camera has taken. A fake Hermès handbag won't have its birth certificate in the official Hermès registry. As we'll see later, the birth certificate for your house is the central hub for its operation and maintenance. A tennis ball won't have a digital birth certificate, but a tennis racquet will. In general, if it has a serial number, it will have a birth certificate online.

One benefit of having metadata online is real-time pricing. Today, pricing engines like CardPricer.com help you learn the value of your baseball trading cards by tracking transactions across the web. In the pull era, every product has an up-to-date market price. Businesses can then make real-time bids on contracts, conduct auctions, look at pricing scenarios from different vendors, etc.

A birth certificate is also a death certificate. When you drink a bottle of wine, you can enter all the information about the taste, whom you shared it with, where, etc. The metadata then goes into the bottle graveyard in your online wine cellar, so you have a complete history of every bottle you've ever consumed (people are already doing this today).

In addition to products, we will syndicate and stream all our media: music, photos, videos, etc. The next several sections describe how those industries will change in the semantic world of the future.

Digital Financial Certificates

We've been using birth certificates in financial assets for thirty years already. In the 1960s, the U.S. securities industry was buried under an avalanche of paperwork as a result of 10 to 12 million shares trading hands per day. The "solution" was to extend the settling time from four days to five and close the exchange early on Wednesdays to let the paperwork catch up to reality. In 1973, the SEC came up with a better idea: stop trading paper certificates. They put all the shares into the newly formed Depository Trust Company and started trading electronic metadata rather than paper. Today, more than 95 percent of all trades are completely electronic, and the DTC holds over $28 trillion worth of paper certificates that never move.

The system now handles *billions* of trades per day and settles most of them on the same day.* Many large companies (AT&T, Microsoft, UPS,

---

*In 2007, over $1.8 *quadrillion* worth of stock was traded using DTC virtual shares that never move.

Intel, Chevron) have now dematerialized *all* their shares, eliminating the paper completely. Registrars handle the ownership links. By the end of 2010, all U.S. exchanges should be 100 percent paperless. In Europe, most exchanges already are.

This trillion-dollar business has already proven the concept of birth certificates and nurseries. Now we just need to extend it to everything else anyone can own.

Catalogs

When you look at a product catalog like Amazon.com in your browser, you're looking at a web page designed to appeal to humans. It describes what the company has, but not in a format the search engines can see easily. Search engines need to guess what's on the page by looking at keywords. The strange part of this is that Amazon's database knows very well what the fields are and what they mean. It gets rid of all that helpful information when displaying the page. For example, if you were to write software to find the price or size of an item on a web page, you'd have to guess which number it is and keep up with any layout changes made to the page, and you have to do that for each web site (this practice is called "scraping").

In the pull era, a catalog is more like a software application than a series of pages with product descriptions and a shopping cart. Product descriptor and pricing information lives in the central repository, where it is semantically tagged and visible to search engines. Product descriptions go into a paper catalog, a web site, your purchasing system, and your phone using special presentation (and possibly viewing) software, similar to that used to view financial reports.

Take a look at **Grainger.com**, a business-to-business catalog containing 800,000 items. Each item is incredibly well specified – you can really imagine this level of detail becoming part of the semantic web. Unfortunately, the catalog *structure* is driven by the software that organizes the paper catalog. The categories seem out of date and make it difficult to find what you're looking for.

Now look at **McMaster.com**, a catalog with over 400,000 items. It seems most of them are available on the front page! If you have good eyesight, it's easy to find what you want on this site, but once you find it, the information isn't in any kind of useful format. It's practically a scan of the page of the paper catalog. Both these businesses live and die by the quality of their metadata, but their legacy thinking is holding them back.

In the not-too-distant future, Grainger could work with a consulting company like Semantic Arts or Top Quadrant to create an ontology of all its products (see Chapter 12). The ontology knows which products satisfy various kinds of (semantically specified) requirements, so it gets smarter and smarter over time. A single big buyer, like a university, can link its own internal ontology to the catalog, and now the magic happens: the Grainger catalog can migrate into the university's planning and purchasing system to help solve problems. The catalog would "know" which products are already installed, make recommendations, give special discounts, and interface with the university's planning software to build what-if scenarios with different products and budgets. No catalog can do that today. Someday, a catalog will be a sophisticated sales tool that can be everything to everyone.

In the semantic future, catalogs will self-assemble on demand. At your request, dozens of systems will come together to help you solve your problem in context. For example, if you're purchasing items for an aircraft, you may be looking for lightweight products. Just ask, and an ad hoc catalog of thousands of lightweight items drawn from dozens of catalogs across the open web will self-assemble to meet your needs. As you add items to your online shopping cart, the information goes to your design space, where you can see the total weight of the plane increase by the exact amount of the products.

Music

Have you been to NIN.com lately? That's where you can stream every single song Nine Inch Nails has ever recorded to your device for free, as many times as you like. That's right – a huge commercial band lets you stream all their songs for free, all day and night. Are they insane? Or could this be the future of music?

It took Apple three years to sell 1 billion songs from its iTunes store, practically wiping out music stores in the same period of time. iTunes really is a virtual record store, imitating the twentieth-century way of purchasing and enjoying music: you download your music files onto your computer and then use it as you would your personal CD collection. You load your MP3 player and take your music everywhere. You pay by the song, and if you want to save a bit of money, you can even buy an album. And don't forget to back up your music files in case you lose them! iTunes may have revolutionized the distribution business, but it didn't change the business model very much.

According to MySpace, it took MySpace Music "a few days" to stream a billion songs after opening their streaming music platform in September 2008. These days, MySpace Music streams about a billion songs a *week,* pays label royalties of 0.4 cents to 1 cent per track, and makes money by selling ads.

In the pull era, most of us won't own any music. We won't even have playlists. We'll just *manage our preferences.* In the pull era, all the music streams to your ears straight from the Internet any time you want it. You have access to every song ever recorded, you never run out of space, you can't lose anything, and some new and interesting (or old and cherished) piece of music is always streaming into your ears, using your **personal music ontology**. Think of it as a personal **Pandora. com** developed just for you, using your tastes and the tastes of others. If you love that smoky lounge vibe by Alex Cortiz, just tag it as a favorite up-tempo beat, and it will mix its way into your music stream whenever you're in the mood. If a friend sends you something you like, your ontology will start to add your friend's ontology to yours (until you change your mind). Your ontology will help you discover music in places you didn't even know about, so you don't even need to keep up with what's happening where – you just need to say whether you like what you hear and keep listening.

Every song lives in a single place (or, more properly, has a unique name) and syndicates from there. There will be a distribution chain, but we only need a single original source for any piece of media, whether it's a blog, a symphony, a sports broadcast, a conference call, a movie, or a song. Once we have a common name space and set of descriptors, every song will be discoverable.

Rhapsody.com is a good example. With Rhapsody, you can get individual songs with ads, radio stations with ads, or unlimited streaming music channels for a subscription fee. You can also use Rhapsody To Go, which lets you store songs and play them on a device; for example, if you go to Antarctica, you could take your music with you. This is called a **tethered download**: it doesn't give you full rights to "own" the song; it just gives you temporary storage of your music stream. Even on a plane flight, you'll either stream your music or preload a few hours' worth and go back to live streaming when your plane lands. If you lose your player, just borrow someone else's and log in.

To see how the music industry will reconfigure, look at television. In the television model, 90 percent of content is free, a tiny percentage is supported by the government and private donations, and the rest, perhaps 9 percent, is paid subscriptions. By the time you read this, the tide will likely have turned and iTunes' monthly music revenues will be in decline. The semantic web signals the end of downloading and owning the rights to any particular song (applications will go web-native a few years later). Soon, 90 percent of music will be streamed for the price of a high-bandwidth connection, supported by advertising, and the music industry will become 90 percent smaller as a result.

Photos and Video

In the pull era, our cameras have memory, but we don't manage it on the camera as we do today. Every picture we take goes straight to the cloud. We've been doing this with our mobile phones for years, of course, but now even high-resolution cameras will do the same trick. If three people are in the photo, the camera can send a separate copy to each person's data locker automatically (see next chapter). Not only is this great for people like me, who have left more than one camera in an airport waiting lounge; it's also important for human rights workers and those who live under repressive governments, who can now ship as they shoot, leaving no film or memory to confiscate. The goal is to reduce the time lag between shooting and sharing to as close to zero as possible, doing most of the processing and uploading at the time of taking the photo.

In the world of pull, we will tag our photos as we go, adding information to help us find them later. For each photo, the semantically aware camera knows:

The date and time

The name of the event, trip, etc.

Where it is

Where the subject of the photo is

The identity of everyone in the photo

Landmarks or other important objects in the photo

Where the photo goes online

Who is to be notified

In the pull era, most people have a small inexpensive camera for shooting birthday parties, but, eventually, many people won't ever need to touch a camera. That's based on the assumptions that most people (1) actually hate dealing with cameras, (2) are terrible photographers, and (3) just want good photos of themselves to magically appear online so they can look at them, share them with friends, and, even though I don't quite understand this behavior, print them onto glossy paper. Only a small percentage of people really enjoy messing with cameras and actually taking and managing photos.

How will you pull photos through without a camera? Simple! Just add your online identifier to something you're carrying on your person (once again, your phone will do nicely), and set it to broadcast the public message "I would like to be photographed." It identifies you anonymously. When you are out in public, people will take photos of you and send them to their own web sites, which then send you a message to come see them (anonymously). You can go to their sites, look them over, and pay whatever the photographer asks for each photo you like. When you buy them, they already come with locations and other people tagged, and they go into your personal data locker.

The Photo Crisis

However we solve the photo crisis, it will be by adding more information to images, because the solution to the overabundance of information is more information.

– David Weinberger

When you and your friends pose in front of any monument, several opportunistic photographers will run up to take your photo.

Those people in the photograph will come home to see a message pointing to the photos. In one day, you could get hundreds of photos taken of you by dozens of photographers you never notice. Fixed cameras sit at obvious points everywhere – simply use your phone to send the nearest camera a message releasing the shutter. You'll see the photo on your phone a second later. That's pull photography – your phone doesn't need a camera to take your picture, it just needs to send the right message. (In the early days, too many photos will be taken with people looking down at their phones to see if the thing is working.) For many people, the best camera will be . . . no camera at all.

You can think of this connected world of photo sharing as an extension of Facebook – it's not really that far from what we have today; it's just that we have to get used to letting other people take our pictures. If you don't want to be photographed, turn that switch off and no one will take any interest. Don't worry about getting ripped off – in the semantic future, no one passing by knows your name or which hotel you're staying in. You're not carrying any cash, and you're certainly not carrying a camera!

If you prefer, bring your camera and don't forget to charge the batteries. Also, don't spend a week at Club Med, where they take your photo all day long and try to sell photos to you that evening after dinner.

In the pull era, just aim your video camera and the signal goes straight to the camera's memory for uploading to the net as bandwidth allows. No more disks, chips, or wires – you can edit or play your video on any display seconds later straight from the Internet. As with photos, this makes human rights workers much safer. Twitter has already shown the political power of real-time metadata and commentary. For video, sites like **LiveLeak.com**, which features up-to-the-minute content, will flourish because the time gap between shooting and viewing is minimized, maximizing the value for the viewer.

> ## Movies

By 2020, the concept of a TV channel is long gone – now you have a virtual VJ (video jockey, similar to a disk jockey) showing a selection of content custom-made for you all the time. It comes from tagged news feeds, interest feeds, friends and family feeds, and previously recorded material. It knows that it's noon and you're eating at your desk. It knows what you've seen and haven't seen. It knows what your friends have seen and liked. Tell it what you're in the mood for, and it will pull the content to you. But when a studio releases a movie, especially a highly anticipated movie, the studio wants to maximize its income in the first month. How will it do that?

The studio could release the film **direct to consumers via the web**, so they can pay half what they pay at the theater and watch it on their home theaters, their laptops, or the airplane display. That's what everyone wants. However, one person can invite twenty friends to come watch, and the studio can't know how many people are in the room. Furthermore, someone could record it and turn his basement into a theater, charging people and taking money away from the studio that funded the project.

If the studio releases **direct to specific devices** at a low price, targeting only portable video players or video phones, it will need a way to be sure those players are secure. This is one of the drawbacks of digital-rights management. If it can be streamed, it can be captured, and if it can be captured, it can be shared. And there's already plenty of incentive to share and resell first-run videos in the gray market. The saving grace is that for mobile phones, the resolution is lower, so the same video will look bad on a larger display. I expect studios will experiment with this approach, but I don't expect it to be mainstream.

Finally, there's the twentieth-century strategy of **selling seats in**

theaters built for the purpose of showing films. I know it sounds crazy, but this is probably the future of big-budget film releases. Movie theaters can deliver the highest-quality experience, sell one seat per ticket, and the pirates won't get a very good copy if they get one at all. There's just too much money at stake in the first month of a film's release to change the game for first-run films.

Theaters won't carry any inventory. They'll just pull movie files directly from the studios' servers. This is already under way. By 2020 it will save hundreds of millions of dollars in prints and shipping.

The Semantic Watch

Now that all our data has migrated online, what will our hardware and software look like? I'll start by asking you to look at your wrist. Think – is the watch on your wrist semantic? What would a semantic watch look like?

Your watch is extremely semantic. It has a controlled vocabulary of seconds, minutes, hours, and perhaps the date. Unfortunately, your watch has no idea what time it is. If you don't set it properly from a reference source, it won't tell you the right time later. The time on all watches in a meeting can vary by a good ten minutes. Change time zones and you must change your watch to match. This is why many people look at their phones to learn what time it is.

The watch of the future may not look different, but inside, things have changed. It's now just another device connected to the Internet. It always shows the accurate time, even in when you're in Nepal. The watch of the future shows even more meaningful information. It's connected to your online life, so it can alert you when you have an important message or appointment. In the pull era, you never tell your watch what time it is – it always tells you. Isn't that what a watch *should* do?

Your Device Mesh

When we are really pulling information, all devices, from your watch to your phone to your laptop to your TV to your video wall to the outdoor JumboTron – are simply displays that connect to the web. Some people call them webtops; others call them netbooks; I call them displays.

The displays we'll use in the pull era won't have an operating system, like Palm or iPhone, Windows or Mac. For a while, smart phones will get smarter, but when the semantic web gets going, you'll prefer to carry a **dumb phone** – a phone that does everything on the web. Within ten years, dumb phones will be much easier to use and manage than smart phones. And they will be infinitely more powerful. Soon, a phone will just be a portable display that, like all displays, simply connects to the web and runs a browser.* The display could be in your pocket, your car, your refrigerator door, your golf cart, or your purse. It could be all of those – you just go from display to display, using your headset to transition from one to the next. It could be *none* of those – to make a call, a wireless headset and access to the Internet are all you need.

There won't be any phone companies providing phone service. We don't need phone service today, and we won't have it tomorrow. All we need is bandwidth – fiber-optic bandwidth at fixed locations and roaming bandwidth when we're on the go. America now ranks fifteenth in broadband penetration among OECD countries. Americans are going wireless in increasing numbers, using the oldest and one of the most outdated wireless networks in the world.† Within ten years, mesh networks and new protocols will move all our communications,

---

* See **Crunchpad.com** for a preview of this kind of device.

† According to an article in the August 15, 2009, issue of *The Economist*, more than 700,000 Americans dropped their landlines each month of 2009. At that rate, the last landline in America will be disconnected in 2025. In Sweden, the national fiber infrastructure lets consumers change broadband providers in under 30 minutes. Australia is investing $30 billion to do the same.

both landline and wireless, onto the web, leaving phone companies (and their bills) behind. As smart phones give way to dumb phones and laptops give way to tablets, all devices will become cheap displays that give you access to the Internet. You'll do everything online, from making phone calls to collaborating with colleagues to building a financial model to recording music to ordering lunch. I'll even go out on a limb and say that within ten years we won't even pay for ring tones and text messages.

Your **device mesh** will be all around you – it will be made of devices you own and many you don't. Get close enough to any device, allow it to recognize you, and it will interact with you as a personal display. Lose or forget your phone? No problem. Grab mine, log in, and my phone instantly becomes yours. Displays will cost pennies; many of them will be free in exchange for doing business with a particular company. Or you'll wear them, fold them, and roll them up. Or they'll self-assemble from smaller displays. Or they'll paint your retina from the frames of your glasses.* Your walls will just be large displays, so be careful if you have kids because that hallway that wasn't there yesterday probably isn't one.

In Chapter 6, I said the bookstore of the future will be a machine that can print any book ever written, but who needs to print books? If you're working in your office, you could be surrounded by walls projecting a nice beach sunset scene, or a live feed of your favorite basketball game on one wall and a live shot of your favorite street in Paris on the other. Your office now looks like an immersive environment of live data feeds, data maps, strategic information, tactical updates, colleagues at work, collaborative workspaces, reference materials, and anything else your online data locker has to tell you. It could completely surround you and it will adapt to your needs.

If you want a book, just click and your walls will turn into the best bookstore in the world, arranged according to your personal ontology.

---

* All these technologies have already been prototyped.

Follow the links to blogs, videos, and movies that all relate to the book you're looking at. When you find something you want to read, you can display it on the entire wall or slide the book onto your flat display* and take it to the bedroom or onto the porch for reading . Your device mesh recognizes you as you move and is always ready to show you what you want, when you want it, no matter where you are.

Whether a device uses a web browser or displays a feed directly from the Internet doesn't matter. Your watch will get updates from a data feed. Your phone already gets sports and stock feeds directly. Today, sports programs are televised with their scores and statistics at the top of the screen, "baked in" to the video signal. In the pull era, statistic feeds, voice commentary, and video feeds are all available separately, so you can put together the view that works best for you.

Although voice dictation and control will continue to gain in popularity, and your wireless earbud will be part of your device mesh, keyboards will still be useful. A semantic keyboard understands context, which means it can change keys according to the user and her needs. A good example is the **Optimus Maximus keyboard** by Lebedev Studio – every key has an LED display that can show anything, from colors to different languages and custom key layouts. It's a piece of adaptive hardware you can actually buy today, and it should come in handy for learning the Dvorak key layout.

Software

As devices get dumber and cheaper, our software will get dumber and cheaper, too. As the semantic web takes shape, the way we work will

---

* Today's electronic book readers are built to save power and manage intellectual property rights. Tomorrow's displays will use new technology like electrofluidic displays, which are just being developed, to show crisper images with less energy, and the tangle of batteries, wires, and transformers will be replaced by wireless power transmission.

change radically. It won't look anything like Mac or Windows. Our collaborative software environments will be much more powerful.

The software we use will all be web-native, in what many people call the web OS. Some people are even calling it Web 4.0, predicting its emergence between 2020 and 2030.* Everything will run between servers and online, and you'll do everything from photo editing to accounting to designing a skyscraper right in the browser. There won't be any more desktop software as we know it today – no one ever wanted to install, back up, maintain, and debug all those programs anyway.†

Applications will break into small, agile modules that come together to perform a particular task, then break up and go back where they came from. The data lockers will handle all the registration, account maintenance, payment, storage, and file issues, so applications just do one thing and do it well. You'll pay for what you use as you use it. Small software companies will flourish in this environment; large companies will spend less on maintenance and have much faster product cycles.

ERP Systems

ERP systems scale wonderfully if you are trying to do more of the same thing you did yesterday.

– Rajat Bhatnagar

Because the file formats include structure (or reference it online), generic software will work across different knowledge domains. The

---

* Nova Spivack, in his blog *Minding the Planet*, defines the third decade of the web (2009–2019) as the infrastructure decade (Web 3.0). The fourth decade (to 2029) will be about agents and the web-based OS (Web 4.0). Learn more at **NovaSpivack.TypePad.com**.

† A pioneering company in this space is JoliCloud, which aims to build the platform I describe here. The company launched just as the manuscript was being finished. Learn more at **Jolicloud.com**.

software for scheduling a table at a restaurant is the same software you use to schedule a seat at a concert, a seat on an airplane, or a room for a business meeting. It's not similar software; it's the *exact same software.* A scheduler doesn't need to know the details of what's being scheduled, because the rules and structure are in the format.

This is **the second level of abstraction of the semantic web:** the structure (a diagram of the restaurant and its tables, or the concert venue, or the airplane seat chart) and rules for working with metadata live somewhere online, where they can be used by all programs that need them. This is what I call data DNA, also called adaptive systems, versus declarative systems, in which the structure and rules are hard-wired into the application itself.

What's Next

In this new world, every piece of meaningful information has an origin – **an authoritative source** – that lives online with a unique name and can only be altered by its creator (or those allowed). This is an important building block to the plug-and-play systems of the future, one that will tear hundreds of billions of dollars of inefficiency out of our economy. As this paradigm starts to become reality, three rules will govern data:

> Each piece of information goes into a container with a unique name.
>
> Each piece of information has a single authoritative source with no copies.
>
> The source of the information dictates the terms of distribution.

In the semantic future, information lives online, waiting to be pulled through your device mesh. If you're watching a movie at home and have to go to the airport, you'll log into the display in the waiting lounge or on the airplane, and the movie will automatically continue where you left off. Your music or favorite news station will start playing as soon as you get into your rental car, because just by opening the door to the rental car, you've logged into your personal data locker and now the rental car (including seat and mirror adjustments) is tuned to your personal ontology. In fact, all your preferences will live online, and your preferences will replace many of the products you own today.

What, exactly, is a personal data locker? I'm glad you asked. Let's find out.

8: Passive Commerce

Pull Concept: The Personal Data Locker

> *There will be thousands of other choices. Your request for a specific movie or television program episode will register and the bits will be routed to you across the network. The information highway will make it feel as though all the intermediary machinery between you and the object of your interest has been removed. You indicate what you want, and presto! you get it.*
>
> – Bill Gates, *The Road Ahead*, 1995

MARKETS ARE MADE OF METADATA: item descriptions, options, prices, availability, locations, offers, responses, and so on. Back in the pre-pull days, if you were looking for something, you had to go to a search engine to get a list of all the web sites with listings and then search each site independently. You could find lots of web sites, but you couldn't find offers. In today's push economy, even though we've made all our documents electronic, we have changed the speed but not the *mechanism* by which buyers find sellers.

This chapter tells the story of consumer pull in a world where everything is connected on the open web using standard formats – a future that doesn't exist yet. In this world, you don't go searching all over for information. You specify what you want, and it finds you.

The Personal Data Locker

Rather than having your information in electronic filing cabinets and on desktop computers, you'll have everything online in your personal data locker. It's the replacement for desktop computers, and it's also the "brain" behind your phone and the rest of the "smart" objects in your life.

The personal data locker stores *all* your information:

All about you

Contacts

Preferences

Descriptions of everything you have

Descriptions of everything you want

Media

Personal records

Travel details

Medical records

Documents and agreements

Financial information

Links

Friends

Memberships and relationships

And so on

For a quick example, go to **SniffTag.com**, a company that makes a dog collar that tells you where your dog has been and builds a history of your dog's outings. Now go to **EyeglassRescue.com**, where you can order a sleeve for your glasses that tells people how to return them to you if you lose them. Rather than keeping all this information on the Sniff Tag and EyeglassRescue web sites, you'll bring it into your central data locker, where you can work with all your data, use all your social networks, and do all your work.

In this chapter, we'll build the personal data locker from the ground up, from your identity and security layers to all the things you'll put in it and all the things you'll do with it. I suggest you skim it first and then come back and read the parts you find most relevant.

Foundation Layer: Identity

A 2001 study showed that 87 percent of the U.S. population can be uniquely identified by just three pieces of information: zip code, birth date, and sex.[19] People trust web sites enough to give all this information many times over, including passwords, and sites like Facebook and MySpace make it public. If it shows up on a web site, even for a day, it can end up in Archive.org forever. We've become used to giving too much information, and the lens of the Internet magnifies it. People manage multiple identities online using sophisticated tools like Post-it notes and their pets' names to remember all their passwords. How many accounts and passwords do you have? How often do you change your passwords?

There's a better way. When you log in to a Google service, as long as you keep using the same browser, you're automatically logged in to all other Google services. That should work across the web, so when you go to web sites where you need a password to enter, you're already logged in. That's called federated log-in or single sign-on. It's the idea behind **OpenID**, an open format for identification that over 50,000 web sites have already agreed to support. OpenID solves the problem of too many log-in names and passwords – it lets you keep one password on one site and use it to open all the locked doors of all the silos around the web.

OpenID lets you log in once in the morning to a trusted site that confirms who you are. From there, you're already logged in to every site that accepts OpenIDs, so you never type another password. The sites you visit (and their tech guys) don't keep any passwords. Now you'll have fewer passwords, and that makes you safer, because you can better manage and more often change a single password. Your personal data locker will probably be the "home base" for your OpenID. Log in there and you're logged in everywhere. (There's a short tutorial on the mechanics of this at **ThePowerofPull.com**.) OpenID is a very thin but very wide layer on the open web. It will allow much more to be built on top of it, as we'll see.

In the pull era, we'll manage our identities better and more safely than we do today. You'll *want* to have an RFID embedded in your business card, to make the information easier for others to use. But the RFID only has your i-name on it, and that's useless to anyone but those you authorize to access your data. An **i-name** is a new standard for identity management that goes on top of OpenIDs and is more powerful. My i-name is **=siegel.** That automatically gives me an identity page online. If you go to that page, you won't see anything, because I haven't allowed you to. But if you ask permission and I grant it, that page will give you the basics for contacting me in a semantic format even your phone can understand – you'll never need to see or know my phone number. A random person going to =siegel will learn less than he can from Googling my full name today, making the *printed* part of the business card more of an identity risk! In fact, many people will have business cards with their company name and i-name only. Call me using my i-name and I'll answer the phone if I want to. If I decide to end the relationship, you will no longer be able to contact me.

You'll sign in to your online data locker with your OpenID. You

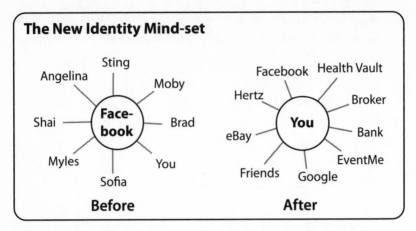

In the push model, the web site is at the center and the people come and go.
In the pull era, you are at the center; web sites get your identity credentials
by permission and authentication, rather than by asking you to fill out forms.

can store all your private information securely in your data locker
and give access to your information following the principle of **least
privilege** – you give out only the information necessary to conduct a
transaction. For example, if I want to purchase a bottle of wine, the
retailer doesn't need to know my age. The retailer needs a trusted third
party to answer the question "Is this buyer the proper age for this
transaction?" This yes/no answer is called a *token*, and the trusted third
party is called a *broker*. Using tokens and brokers, all parties involved
in any transaction reveal information in stages, even anonymously,
able to exit the deal with the least amount of information exchanged
if necessary.

Eventually, your ID stack will have all your government-issued documents as well: birth certificate, immunization record, driver's license, or-
gan donor card, library card, passport, work permit, marriage license, and
death certificate. These successive layers of identity and personal details
also have successive levels of security around them, so you only reveal
what's appropriate to each party:

Personal

Most trusted people

Family

Friends

Associates, colleagues

Business partners

The public (strangers)

These are **foundation layers**. They are under your control at all times. I-names are ready to help you control your identity now. (Learn more about i-names at **inames.net**.)

> ### Action Layer: Card Selectors

My guess is that you've typed your name, address, and credit card number into a web form more than a few times. Using your personal data locker, you'll set up prepackaged modules called **i-cards** and then apply them to your transactions, rather than doing all that work by hand each time. Whether you are buying a bottle of wine (which requires age verification), registering for a political rally, buying a mobile phone, or joining a diet program, your data locker is your virtual assistant, helping you do everything easily using i-cards.

An i-card is a complete set of credentials and instructions for a given purpose. Different software vendors use the same standards, defined by the **Information Card Foundation**. Some of them look very much like the cards you have in your wallet. One of them looks a lot like your passport. Underneath, there are common exchange standards, so you can use these virtual cards the same way you use the real cards. They all work with your OpenID and your i-name, and they can also handle password management. There are three types of these cards already in use:

Personal i-cards are for personal identification. These cards live in your data locker, so you can use them in the real world as you use your cards today – to buy tickets, enter your building, go to the gym, buy a cup of coffee, or open your garage door. You may build a personal i-card to manage all your passwords, or you may want to manage them individually.

Action cards perform tasks in prepackaged scenarios. You can make action cards for repetitive tasks, like buying wine or making doctor appointments. They hold *all* your tickets and passes (described later in this chapter). Use one to register for a hotel room online, and on the appropriate day that same i-card will guide you to your room, unlock the door, set the room temperature, and make sure your favorite TV show is on the display. Use another to find and start a rental car or even a friend's car (with permission).

Managed or provisioned cards are for government and work-related business. Managed i-cards will be branded and come with certain restrictions; they represent a contract between you and the organization. AAA has one for discounts. Equifax has one for age verification. By the time you read this, there will likely be hundreds of i-cards for different purposes. Microsoft, Novell, and others already provide free **i-card selectors** that let you store all your i-cards in one place. In time, i-cards will replace all our physical identification cards, medical-alert bracelets, passports, voter registrations, security clearances, and work-related identity documents.

The Government Services Administration (GSA) has already launched an impressive pilot project to experiment with i-cards. You can use your government-issued i-card to let you in to a government demonstration web site, showing that your identity and security levels are preserved. By the time you read this, that project might already have turned into a working system for interacting with various government agencies. (Learn more at **InformationCard.net**.)

Identity 3.0

This new world of identity tools is called **Identity 3.0.** Identity 1.0 was the world of physical documents, ID cards, signatures, and fingerprints. Identity 2.0 was user names and passwords on dozens of web sites and services. We've already seen some of the Identity 3.0 tools – OpenIDs, i-names, and i-cards. These are the basic principles of Identity 3.0:

Online, you are in the center; web sites and services cluster around you. You are always logged in.

Fewer passwords are *better*, because they are more manageable and can be changed more often. Of course, you can have as many passwords as you like.

Using the principle of least privilege, both parties to a transaction reveal information in stages, as necessary.

Third-party brokers will help us engage with others without giving away sensitive information.

You can authorize third parties to do only the things you want them to do on your behalf and nothing else.

You create as many identities as you want; each identity gives you access to its own services and communities.

Government-issued identifiers are for dealing with governments only and are not for civil affairs.

The new tools help prevent phishing, fraud, identity theft, and other common cyber crimes.

Contacts

As I've explained, your i-name opens your personal data locker. All your personal information lives in one place and never moves. How do you connect to friends and colleagues?

Since this is passive commerce, you do it passively, which is to say you don't do it at all. To build your personal contact list, you *don't* enter the names, addresses, and phone numbers of your friends. You don't even have to know what they are. Instead, you simply add people to your friend list by i-name. Your contact list, in all its glorious detail, might look something like this:

First	Last	I-Name
David	Siegel	=siegel
Robert	Reich	=robert.reich
Kaliya	Hamlin	=kaliya
George	Soros	=georgesoros
Moby		=moby
Sofia	Coppola	=sofia

I'm leaving out how you met and any personal notes, but I'm not leaving out phone numbers, addresses, email addresses, or birth dates (the equal sign is required, but the periods are just a convention). All that information is in the person's personal data locker, and he or she has given you permission to access it. To call Moby, just touch or click his name on your phone. If Moby has allowed you to call through, his phone will ring. If not, he may let new callers leave a message or ring his assistant. If Moby changes his phone number, you won't have to know, because phone numbers are a thing of the past.* In the

---

* Eventually, there won't be any phone numbers; we'll all use net-based naming schemes. In the meantime, the phone numbers are completely hidden – you never give one out and never have to remember yours or anyone else's. For a preview of how this works today, visit **voice.google.com.**

world of pull, you don't manage the details; you manage the relationships. If everyone maintains his or her own contact information, the entire system reduces to its most ruthlessly efficient. This "first level of abstraction" – associating unique names with contact information – is like having Facebook contacts at web scale, built into our phones and everything else all the time.

Want to send me a package? Once the shipper project turns into reality (Chapter 3), you'll just write =siegel on any letter or box and drop it in the mail. The postal service gets my current address from my personal data locker and my schedule on an as-needed basis. If you write your i-name on the return address, my data locker will handle the details from there, because it knows if I'm expecting the package and where I want it to go. When I check into my next hotel, your package is waiting for me (if that's what I want). You may pay for the shipping, but I *pull* the package to me. (This should save a little money – the U.S. Postal Service forwards, returns, or destroys more than 5 *billion* pieces of mail per year as a result of incorrect addresses.[20])

Haves

Your personal data locker will include a section for your personal inventory. Everything of value you own has an ownership link in your personal data locker that links to its birth certificate somewhere on the semantic web (think names, not locations). Things you own yourself are on one list; other things you share with people (family members, friends, clubs, etc.) are linked to lists of joint ownership.

To get your personal inventory started, imagine you're a watch collector, and you have a platinum Patek Philippe Calatrava Travel Time, Ref. 5134, you bought in 2005 while on a ski holiday in Davos (it was a good year). You go to the online product description atlas and search for that exact model until you find its description. Since the company doesn't have digital birth certificates online yet, you make your own.

Start with the generic description people have entered into the atlas, and add:

Date and time of purchase

Purchased from

Serial number

Condition when purchased

Condition history

Strap/bracelet/clasp/buckle info

Special features

Any engraving or special markings

Any modifications

Ownership history

Service history

Photos (with dates)

Location (city, not closet!)

How much you would sell it for

Etc.

You do this for each watch, and now your collection is online. If you ever sell that particular watch, you transfer the metadata to the new owner.

This applies to everything you own. Anything of value goes into the "haves" section of your online data locker – generally durable goods that have serial numbers. Because your inventory is now online, you benefit from having it in standard formats all software can see. You can make your inventory as public or private as you like.

Your personal inventory affects other areas of your data locker. The present value of everything you own goes into your personal balance sheet and updates continuously. When you acquire a new item of value, it's included in your homeowner's insurance policy, which adjusts automatically. If your house burns to the ground, all your *original documents* – precious photos, signed contracts, records, and a list of everything you own – are still online in good shape. Your artwork may not survive, but its replacement value has already been calculated. To file an insurance claim, just have your house burn down and everything starts automatically.

Passive Commerce

An unlikely but instructive example: suppose you have spent enough time with your data locker to describe everything you own, using standard descriptors that the search engines can see and understand. Suppose one of those things happens to be a 1956 silver Mercedes-Benz 300SL Gullwing Coupe you bought a long time ago for $80,000 and personally refurbished (including, of course, a set of fitted luggage for the back seat). A pricing tool surveys recent sales and tells you that today the car is worth around $600,000. (The current value of all your items, and your entire balance sheet, is a by-product of market information on the open web.) But you don't want to sell it, so your "sale price" field says $1.5 million, because if someone wants to give you that much, you'll take it. You also put a "rental price" of $50,000 per day, for the same reason. You do this with all the cars in your collection, and that makes your collection visible to other potential buyers, without your having to list it on any special web sites. At those prices, you don't get any offers, but other collectors can see your car and put it on their wish list if they like.

Now, it happens that a production company is shooting a film in your neighborhood. The prop guy sees your car online and offers you $120,000 to rent the car for a week as a prop, insured. So you take it. Later, you decide you want to sell your beloved car because you've found something else that's stolen your heart. You simply lower the "sale price" to $750,000. Now your car starts to show up on the radar of other collectors, and you start to see a few inquiries coming in. Drop the price further and your in-box starts to fill up quickly. When you sell the car, the metadata goes to the new owner, your name goes into the ownership history, and you immediately stop getting offers.

The personal data locker is your command-and-control hub; from it, you can pull offers from around the world to a single, central "dashboard" without going to any web sites. You could even hold auctions right from your own personal data locker just by pressing the START AUCTION button on a description of something you own.

As I write, the term "passive commerce" is not yet in Wikipedia, but it will be. It does significant damage to companies that charge for wholesale and retail listings. And it doesn't just work for what I call the long long tail of consumer leftovers.* In the world of pull, the open web is the marketplace, data lockers present supply and demand, search engines do the work, and the listings are free.

Wants (Reverse Search)

How did the person looking for your car find it? How will you find what you are looking for? Your online data locker also has a section where you list all the things you want. Start by going to the online

---

* The long tail is all the products and content people are trying to sell today. The *long long tail* is all that, plus everything people don't bother to try to sell because it's too difficult or expensive to create a listing.

product atlas to find descriptions of the things you're looking for. Then just fill out product descriptions in reverse, specifying not exact information but *ranges*:

Models

Age range

Acceptable options

Materials

Colors

Sizes

Price range

Location distance

Etc.

As a watch collector, I'm always on the lookout for a Langematik Perpetual, Ref 310.025, in platinum, of course. They only make about 100 of these every year, and they are highly coveted, so keeping an eye on eBay to see if one shows up isn't a high-percentage strategy. There are dozens of sites I'd have to watch. By broadcasting my desire on the open web, those few owners of this watch can instantly see their market.

You can list everything you're looking for in the "wants" section of your online data locker. Once we specify everything semantically, using an appropriate descriptor, our software agents can look for things online or the search engines can make the matches and bring us the results. Nonprofits can list the items they need and the benefits of giving.

The same goes for services. I can say I'm looking for a new tax lawyer. There will be a standard format for describing tax lawyers on the open web, and **webs of trust** to help me specify who sees my request. My "wants" can be local or global. I only set them up once and turn them off when I find what I'm looking for (or when it finds me).

Point of Purchase

Did you think I was going to ask you to enter complete descriptions of all the products you own by hand? It won't be long before manufacturers will start including online birth certificates with products and the transaction will switch the ownership automatically. The birth certificate will live on the manufacturer's server, and then link to your personal data locker. Even if you buy a home or an airplane, signing the digital receipt to release the money will automatically set the ownership link to your personal data locker. You'll see the description of the item online, work with it during the life of the product, or transfer the metadata to someone else later when you sell the product.

There are certificates for services as well as products. Need to return something? The digital birth certificate is tailor-made for the return merchandise authorization (RMA) process. You can check the status of your repair or replacement at any time because the metadata reflects what's happening in the real world. You can watch a complicated RMA process as it goes through all the steps necessary for your product's repair and be notified of decisions you need to make along the way. Certificates for services performed on anything of value will have their place in its online birth certificate.

Tickets and Passes

Have I mentioned that in the pull era, data doesn't move? In this future, every seat at every event, or on every airplane, bus, train, or helicopter, is a digital birth certificate in a standard format. I didn't say every ticket *has* a birth certificate – I said it *is* one. All tickets now live online in one place and never move, even long after the event has taken place. Anything you use to validate a ticket is simply an artifact – it could be a paper ticket with a bar code, an i-card on your phone, an RFID tag, even your own iris. This may sound creepy, but it isn't. For example, I'll walk into an event at Oakland's Coliseum with my phone on, and the turnstile will send a request to my online data locker, looking for the ticket. I'll see the request on my phone, acknowledge it (with a password if necessary), and the venue's system will allow me to enter. In most cases, I won't give my identity; I just need to prove I own the ticket. My phone will then guide me to my seat. In the same way, I'll open my hotel room door or get into my rental car and tell it to start.

Tickets can come with preferences. A ticket to a gala dinner can point to your health profile, which says you're allergic to shellfish, and the staff will know where you're sitting – if you want them to. A ticket can have a preapproved "not to exceed" amount for extra expenses. A hotel reservation can know your temperature settings, minibar preferences, media preferences, etc.

Suppose you purchase a ticket for a flight to London. Your online data locker points to that ticket, and you can see your seat in the plane's layout online. Search engines like Yahoo will see *every seat on every flight for the next twelve months*. Have you ever tried to build a map of all the trips you've ever taken? It's tough to do from memory, and who saves all his ticket stubs? In the pull era, *the tickets themselves* tag our data lockers as we fly, leaving a semantic contrail of cities and buildings visited, photos taken, things we've bought, people we've met, and so forth.

NOTE: Passes aren't tickets. Passes will have their own standard data format and will allow access according to the terms of the contract. A pass is a means of authentication to enter a location for a certain period of time. Just come and go, and the system will let you in as long as you're still allowed. A ski pass will log all your vertical feet, record which lifts you took, and link to your ski history online.

Vertical Domains

In addition, your locker has room for all your **vertical domain documents**. You can add as many areas and subareas to your data locker as you like. For example, if you're active in golf, into ski racing, on a baseball team, and go bowling once a week, all those specialized scoring and training formats will live in the sports domain of your data locker.

All your tickets, receipts, memberships, car mileage, and every record of everything you've done will live here in the appropriate area. Search this database by date, trip, category, amount, etc. Every piece of paper you have ever put into a filing cabinet (or intended to) lives here in your personal data locker. Family and work areas will have all their own documents and tools as well.

The Personal Ontology

I'll define ontologies more fully in Chapter 12, but for now, an ontology is just a long list of statements that we know to be true, each in the form of triple statements, like these:

I	like	Esquivel
I	love	lounge music
Esquivel	belongs to	lounge music

Put enough of these together and you have a model of what you like and don't like, even if you can't specify it semantically yourself. There are times when you don't know what you want exactly, and there are times when a pleasant surprise will substitute nicely for whatever you thought you wanted.

Your personal data locker will store your personal ontology. It helps you find television shows and movies, it helps you learn about wines you might enjoy, it helps you find bargains online, plan a trip, find events you might want to attend, or spot a new restaurant, and it can help with your dating life if you're single. Hook it to your everyday activities and you'll build an ontology with millions of triples, all of which make your data locker into a "smart" virtual assistant that continues to learn as you go through your day.

Your personal ontology knows what size you are, what you already have, what you buy, and what you don't buy. It knows what you bought for yourself and what you bought for your nephew. Just walking around town, your ontology can steer you toward something or someone you might otherwise have passed up. It knows if you're left-handed, what sizes to buy for your niece, what allergies you have, and what kind of dark chocolate you prefer. If all your friends have their personal ontologies online, you'll collaboratively find a new restaurant or movie you all want to try but haven't yet. The more you use your data locker, the more it extends your eyes and ears to places you never would have noticed. It's always under your control, acting as your personal helper, not your alter ego.

Whether you're looking for a company to acquire or a good electrical contractor, your work ontology will help guide the virtual software agents that scan the infosphere, working with you to fine-tune your likes and dislikes. Many people will contribute to a group or company ontology, eliminating much of the back-and-forth messaging we do today just to coordinate tasks and preferences.

Do you remember the great Italian restaurant you loved when you were last in Florence? Think you can find it using Google? Probably not. But you were there and you paid with your credit card, didn't you? Think of all the semantic **informational and transactional exhaust** you leave behind every day. If your ontology picks it up and you just add a bit more information (like whether you enjoyed the restaurant, or the wine, or the band, or had a problem with a salesperson, etc.), you'll find the restaurant by mining your own personal history. As you answer emails, delete spam, look at photos, specify wants and haves, or listen to music, your ontology is always looking over your shoulder, learning. (We'll see more of this build-as-you-go approach in Chapter 12.)

Your ontology will become a key asset. You won't want to be without it, and you won't want others to use it against you. That's why I hope you won't mind paying a monthly fee for your do-it-all data locker, because if you pay for it you'll know you will always control it. If Google or Microsoft offers you a free data locker, ask how portable your data will be when you want to take it elsewhere later.

Mass Customization

The personal data locker is your portal to a world of custom-made products, via the standard descriptions and measurements any program can understand. Many companies have been able to customize products for years already. The missing link has been the ability to integrate the data into the production line. From ordering sneakers to stopping arthritis to finding a compatible kidney online, your personal ontology will be hard at work plugging into various systems. Clothing and sizes will be an early success – consumers now say that fit is their number two influence on purchase (after style).[21]

Your body scan, models of your feet and hands, even a biometric profile of how you move will be part of your online data locker. Who needs to go to a store? Just upload your personal ontology and try out clothes, build a desk, or order ski boots while sitting in bed. Your personal data locker can give out your specifics, even an orthotic prescription, so suppliers can make or customize the product for you.

Preferences

Any device you use can simply keep its preferences inside your data locker and access it as necessary. Let's take the example of a mattress.

A mattress will be an active surface that can respond to your body according to a preset ontology (note that I didn't say "program"). If you roll on your side, it can become softer just under your shoulders. On your back, it can be stiff as a board. It recognizes who you are, and it may be able to recognize the other person in the bed. (That has some interesting consequences – good thing we can set up different identities and give each one its own data locker!) The bed can tell when you're not sleeping and has settings for other kinds of activities. Like reading!

You set up your sleep ontology using software that doesn't know much about sleep and doesn't need to. It just watches you sleep and tries things, and then it sends you an email in the morning and asks how you slept last night. Just by answering, you'll improve your sleep for the next night, and it changes with your needs. If you're injured, the mattress will learn what's most comfortable and adjust as necessary.

Now, *any* mattress is your mattress! Use your phone to enter the hotel room and – voilà! – the bed program is already driven by your personal ontology. No matter where you sleep, if the mattress uses the standards and is online, you're in your own comfortable bed, just the way you want it. Believe it or not, blankets will do the same thing. What about pillows? The programmable pillow that helps prevent snoring already exists and will be out commercially in a few years.[22]

Both mass customization and preferences will be part of our data lockers after we've built the proper infrastructure. It will probably start in commercial orders and migrate to consumers sometime between 2020 and 2030.

Job Searches

One small part of your online data locker is your résumé. Soon, it will be the only one you'll ever need. In the old days, your résumé was printed in a nice typeface like Garamond on off-white cotton paper. The process of finding a job took weeks or even months. Today, in the push economy, you fill out a different form on each web site, or you email a Word attachment in any typeface you like, as long as it's Times New Roman. Advanced candidates send PDF documents. It takes several days just to fill out all the forms on all the recruiting web sites.

In the pull era, things have changed a bit. You start by adding your universal résumé to your online data locker once and once only. You can also fill out several standardized assessment modules that answer more in-depth questions for various jobs, and there is now a standardized set of skill descriptions. You can't go all the way in providing exactly the information a hiring manager might need to give you a job, but you can answer the most common questions to get through the screening process and set up an interview using your online calendar. All these modules scream through the hiring infrastructure because the formats are native.*

Over the next few years, all résumé-listing sites will allow standardized résumés to become feeds, so you can add your résumé to a dozen job databases with twelve clicks. You indicate your level of interest in a new job on a scale from 0 ("happy where I am, thanks") to 9 ("can start tomorrow"). You also indicate your desired salary range, location, travel, seniority level, and so on. Then you do nothing, and the interview offers come to you.

Did I say twelve clicks? The pull power shift will turn those twelve clicks into a single click. Just put your résumé into your data locker and let it work from there. The search engines now replace the recruiting sites. To actively look for a job, just indicate that you're more interested in finding a job today than you were yesterday (change that one number from 0 to 6, for example). Now interview offers start coming in and

---

* The first universal résumé is the **hResume microformat**, which is very lightweight but at least it's a start. Today, over 9 million people already have hResumes online, mostly thanks to LinkedIn, which adopted and promotes the format. Eventually, a stronger résumé format will emerge, perhaps based on HR-XML, which is used in many back-office human resources applications today.

your professional ontology filters them according to your priorities. If you take a job, just move that slider back to "not looking" and your name immediately drops off the screens of dozens of recruiters. You do all this even more anonymously than you could back in the old world of push.

When the semantic vocabularies get going, we'll have standard descriptors for schools, degrees, companies, and skills (standards groups are working on these; Facebook's database is already disambiguating school names for hundreds of millions of people). You'll link more of your résumé to specific descriptors online, rather than just typing text into fields. Then the entire résumé will be live, semantic, and on the web. It will *build itself* when you go to school and accept a job, and it will *update itself automatically* as a by-product of getting grades and doing your job.

Wills

We can now see how your personal data locker comes to life using the example of your death. In the old days, you wrote a will by hand, typed it out, or had a lawyer write it for you. You mailed several copies to relatives and one to your lawyer. These people had to interpret and execute your wishes after you died. In today's world of online convenience, you just go to LegalZoom.com, fill out the questions, and they put your paper will in the mail within 48 hours. Isn't that progress?

That was back in 2010. In the pull era, everything you own is already listed in your personal data locker. All your relatives have personal data lockers online as well. Your will is now a live, *executable* document that lets others pull your assets to them according to your wishes. The paper copy you hold in your hands is simply an artifact. If you move or sell your house, the will updates automatically. If the laws change, your will responds. Your health records reflect your death details, and your personal information remains online for researchers to learn about you and see your place in the online family tree. If an heir dies first, your online will adjusts accordingly, even emailing you with any questions. People assigned various tasks can certify that they have been done. Your will continues to carry out your wishes – possibly for many years – after you die.

What's Next

The data locker is a secure online account that holds or links to many containers, both horizontal (identity) and vertical (activity, industry). Standard formats for metadata and i-cards will form the reusable building blocks we'll use to assemble documents and perform tasks. The i-cards will work with brokers to give out only as much identity information as needed for a given task. Then the software agents of passive commerce can really go to work for us.

Could a data locker possibly work in the world of commercial purchasing, where professional buyers spend all day working on complicated orders? It can, and it will. It's already happening today at sites like FindRFP.com. I'll have to save this case study for a few years, but eventually the corporate data locker will create new markets for commercial goods and services.

Once we are pulling information, the line between passive and active will blur. It will be hard to tell whether you are looking for something or it is looking for you. The open web connects the dots directly, eliminating the metadata middlemen.

Just to be clear: **the online data locker will *replace* today's laptop and desktop computers and their operating systems**. It will replace all the hard drives in our lives. It will be the interface for your work, your personal life, your games, your camera, your phone, refrigerator, bed, and television. I can't say when, but I'm willing to bet the transition will be over well before 2030. The race is on. Keep up with the latest developments at **ThePowerofPull.com**.

9: The Home of the Future

Pull Concept: Product Life-Cycle Management

News is what someone wants to suppress. Everything else is advertising.

– Alfred Harmsworth (Lord Northcliffe)

MY FRIEND WADE AND I are walking into the Urban Planning Exhibition Hall in Shanghai's People's Square. In a room the size of a basketball court is a scale model of the city of Shanghai as it is scheduled to look in 2020. There are thousands of buildings. Clear plastic models denote future projects, and there are many of them.

The scale model of Shanghai took tens of thousands of hours to build. Walking around it from the viewing track, however, I can't help but wonder how much of it is already inaccurate. It's a great tourist attraction, but, now that it's built, the model plays no role in the day-to-day activities of urban planners.

In this chapter, we'll follow future homeowner Nina as she buys, owns, and sells a home, dealing with all the semantic information it produces. We'll see how the metadata market for buying and selling homes will change in response. Even though I'll use home ownership as a deep example of how all the previous concepts come together, these principles could just as easily apply to your industry. Managing the product cycle from birth to use to reclamation is called **product life-cycle management**.

We'll start with the production of a refrigerator and watch it take its place in the new home.

The Refrigerator

A new company makes a **thermoelectric cooler**, a solid-state heat pump on a chip that will soon replace all the liquid-condenser cooling units in air conditioners and refrigerators. Each chip has a tiny RFID circuit embedded in it and a birth certificate online.

A refrigerator company uses a collaborative workspace to design the first refrigerator with a thermoelectric cooler. To make everything fit, all the suppliers produce virtual parts that together build a 3-D model of the appliance. Each part does what its real-world counterpart does, so the designers can run the virtual refrigerator and see how it performs, check it for noise and vibration, and so on. When the final design moves into production, the pull-based system collates the orders and, in turn, orders thousands of parts from dozens of vendors to make the first production run of refrigerators.

Each part in each refrigerator has its own digital birth certificate. The virtual model of the factory controls what happens inside the real factory. Every single part checks in with the system when it arrives (via RFID) and is assigned a place in the virtual factory as well as in the real one. If a part doesn't arrive as scheduled, the virtual system reconfigures to accommodate before there's a backup on the production line. Everyone can see the virtual inventory and process flows on huge displays around the factory.

Back to the chip manufacturer, who sends chips out to dozens of factories. Unfortunately, two days' worth of production is spoiled by a problem with the material, and it's too late – the chips have shipped. Some have gone to the refrigerator manufacturer, some to a car air-conditioning manufacturer. Each individual chip in that run can be stopped on arrival and returned, even as new chips are air-freighted overnight to replace them. And the systems at each factory (or even en route to the dealer) compensate accordingly.

Dassault Systèmes

Dassault Systèmes is a leader in product life-cycle management. The company makes proprietary platforms for creating 3-D models in automotive design, manufacturing, product design, architecture, and more. The models are getting smarter all the time, going from sketch to design to manufacturing. It will take time before the data formats are open and standard, but spending time on the Dassault web site will help bridge the gap between this chapter and reality. I encourage you to visit their site and see the vision emerging. Learn more at **3ds.com**.

The dealer sells only the good refrigerators, and their birth certificates link to the new owners' data lockers, which each has an area dedicated to home management, where the refrigerator's metadata will go. The refrigerator chip sends a stream of information to the virtual house online, coordinating with the thousands of temperature sensors throughout the house to optimize the use of all heating and cooling devices (to the food, the refrigerator is a cooling device; to the house, it's a heat source). Each device has its own identity, and this lets the owner see a dashboard of total energy use in the home, broken down by appliance, heating and cooling cycles, day-night, room, season, etc.* (In the pull era, no one ever comes to read an electrical meter.)

The virtual house sends information back all the way to the chip supplier, so the manufacturer has visibility to all its chips as they work. This lets the chip company learn how customers use the products, spot prob-

---

* Google is working on the information infrastructure for consumer energy consumption. Learn more at **Google.org/powermeter.**

lems, and make improvements. Based on information from the chip company, the refrigerator manufacturer can update the programming of every refrigerator installed via the Internet, making all installed refrigerators more efficient. As always, the system shields everyone's identity and maintains permissions. When it's time to repair or replace the cooling unit, the product life-cycle management system helps refurbish or recycle all the components.

More and more, the virtual world controls the real world. Lights, windows, and heat pumps connect to temperature sensors, so when it's sunny in a room, the lights and heaters can dim in the right places, preventing overheating and saving money. This practice, called **harvesting daylight**, saves up to 30 percent of the cost of lighting a commercial building. New systems are doing the same with outside airflow and temperature.*

Refrigerators adjust their temperature according to their contents. Rooms adjust their own conditions according to use patterns and predictions.† Homes can cooperate to use their appliances at staggered times, preventing over-peak loads at power plants, keeping energy prices low. As product life-cycle management matures, a product like a refrigerator will become both a producer and consumer of information.

Product life-cycle management is already a $15 billion business, with major companies like Siemens and Oracle heavily invested. The data standards and birth certificates I describe in this book will bring all these separate steps – manufacturing, sales, service, and recycling – together into an ecosystem that cooperates like never before.

---

* Designers are now learning to use the pressure and temperature differentials on the sunny and shady sides of buildings as power sources and pumps, to move air in and out of a building. Mesh networks of RUBEE chips on the outsides of buildings will be able to adjust the air flow precisely, even in response to a passing cloud. Come to **ThePowerofPull.com**, where I'll track green-building innovations and the metadata they need to operate on a new scale of efficiency.

† Remember, your home knows your calendar, so if you're gone for the weekend and coming back Sunday night, it can adjust the temperature automatically, *without guessing.*

Building a Home

The developer who built the house starts the project as a virtual space online, where an architect first sketches and then builds a 3-D model of how the home will look. When the client approves the overall "envelope" design, the architect puts accurate dimensions on the walls, doors, and negative spaces for appliances and cabinets. At this point, the designers run simulations of variables like sunlight, shadow, wind, temperature, and views. Specialists add the framing and structural details, then the infrastructure for plumbing, ventilation, electrical, communication, lighting, and so forth. Then a team of designers specifies all the interior elements: cabinets, appliances, windows, lights, and surfaces. Everything is semantic, so the information "plugs in" and fits together. Designers can build what-if scenarios to look at different approaches to various problems. The bids come in virtually, so the client sees how much the current design will cost at current prices.

BIM

The language for constructing the virtual home is the building information management (BIM) standard. BIM is a set of processes and standards for managing building informatics, from design and construction through maintenance and improvement. BIM helps create a more integrated design, reduces errors, finds conflicts, helps locate the sources of problems, enforces compliance with regulations, and much more. Although relatively new, BIM has good momentum in the design community and among software developers.

The real estate developer shows the new virtual house to the customer, and it is in this context that the customer looks at, compares, and chooses appliances, floors, windows, colors, etc. In this marketing environment, the client decides between competing offers for all the choices. After the client makes final decisions and approves the final price, construction begins.

Now a series of semantic legal documents and payments manages the process. The order for the refrigerator goes through to the manufacturer. During construction, every fixture, appliance, door, and cabinet has a preprogrammed arrival place in the house, determined by a semantic location code. If there are changes during the building process, all the software responds. As the home is built, progress information goes to the urban planning office and the various inspectors. It's impossible to say whether the metadata tracks the real world or drives it.

Owning a Home

When new homeowner Nina takes delivery of the house, she gets the keys to the front door (actually, a new i-card shows up in the i-card selector on her mobile phone). The system that sketched, designed, and constructed the house now switches the ownership link to her online data locker, where it becomes her living documentation and control center. Nina can monitor her energy expenditure, work with the adaptive lighting schemes and environmental settings, respond to the home's request for maintenance, and much more.

Nina's new house doesn't have thermostats as we know them. Instead, there are dozens of sensors in every room, and now she can look at a thermal map of the home and make sophisticated adjustments to the heating system, even taking the wind and sun into account. If she has extra energy, she can sell it back to the highest bidder on the grid. In summer, the house stores energy at night for use during the peak afternoon hours.

The appliances are smart, putting out information as well as heating, cooling, and light. When the furnace filter needs replacing, the furnace can detect it, sending her a request for a new filter, which she can approve. When the washing machine needs replacing, she'll see a list of bids to supply a new machine that will fit in that exact space and meet the needs of the use pattern recorded in her home's data locker.

There are displays all over the house – if Nina realizes she needs something, she can just enter it the moment she thinks of it and the item shows up on her "wants" list. She'll see that list when she's at the grocery store, or she can press a button on her phone and have the grocery store deliver the items on her list any time.

All this metadata and feedback speeds up cycle times throughout the industry, because researchers can use real aggregate data rather than sample data. For example, during a big storm, it's easy to see a city map of all the rooms where temperature drops quickly, indicating possible window damage, on a minute-to-minute basis. This kind of information will help us design the next generation of cities, houses, windows, and doors better and faster.

When the environment provides the information to help you do what you want, it's called **ambient intelligence**. With standard semantic formats, we'll hook all these signals up and send them to the "control center" for your home. It's not a room or a computer, it's the home management facet of your online data locker.

Remember the RUBEE chips I mentioned in Chapter 4? Sometime in the middle of this century, you'll be able to go to the hardware store and pick up a bucket of autonomous **robotic ants.** You'll let them go in your building and they'll explore the space in the walls, sending messages back wirelessly, taking photos, making videos, repairing their own network as some of them get trapped or stop working. Within a few days, you'll have a complete map and images of everything inside the walls of your building. The robots will haul wires or fiber-optic cables, patch broken pipes, find and repair electrical problems, and more. Then you'll call them and most of them will go back into the bucket (the rest will turn themselves off). You'll control them from a panel in your online data locker.

Nina's electric car sits in her garage, charged up from the night before. It has a touch-screen display on the dashboard, and the display has the owner's manual on board as an e-book that comes straight from her online data locker. The owner's manual is not a PDF from the time the car was made – it's a document that is always up to date. In fact, all the owner's manuals for all her products are sitting in her online data locker. Isn't that cool?

No. That's the push model again. In the pull era, there are no owner's manuals. There are living systems that help Nina solve problems. If the car has a problem or the roof leaks or the TV won't turn on, she tells her data locker what the problem is and *the data locker interacts with the product directly*, solving the problem or getting the help she needs, courtesy of the semantic web. Whatever it took to fix the problem will go back to the manufacturer to help make its products better.

Plumbing will still be a messy job done by guys toting wrenches, but there's a tremendous amount of information involved in the plumbing of the future. Today, we treat our water far from the point of use and lose half of it along the way. Later in this century, many buildings and homes will have to monitor, clean, and possibly recycle their own water supply, aided by the information flowing into their owner's data locker.

Selling a Home

Years later, Nina takes a job in another city; she wants to sell her home. Does she need a realtor?* Should she try to sell it herself? Can her online data locker help? In the next few sections, we'll look at the metadata and processes for selling homes. Let's start back in 2009.

In the United States, about $1 trillion worth of homes changes hands in an average year. Seven hundred thousand professional realtors average six home sales per year each, work an average of forty hours per

---

* It's supposed to be REALTOR®, but for editorial reasons and consistency I'll stick with realtor. All trademarks are property of their individual owners.

deal, and collect an average $12,600 in commissions per sale, for about $50 billion in commissions.

The main selling tool of the National Association of Realtors (NAR) is the multiple listing service (MLS) network. The MLS started as a physical book of photocopied forms and photos. Realtor.com presents an electronic subset of those forms. Each of the 900 separate and independent U.S. markets has its own format and vocabulary. The software for each market is built around local terms and customs.

Realtors have enjoyed a near monopoly on listings and sales, with fixed commissions of 6 to 7 percent nationwide. The FSBO (for sale by owner) market remains around 15 to 20 percent of homes sold. Even though those listings include sales to friends and relatives, sites like ForSaleByOwner.com, Owners.com, and Craigslist continue to grow. But the playing field is tilted. While realtors make good use of resources like Trulia and Craigslist, owners without realtors have no access to the MLS.

Separate studies from Northwestern University and Stanford found that FSBO sellers are as effective as agents in maximizing the sales price of their homes. After commissions, the studies reported, sellers who sell "by owner" keep more money than sellers who sell through agents. In his book *Freakonomics*, Steven Levitt cites a study of 100,000 homes sold in Chicago showing that realtors keep their own homes on the market an average ten days longer and sell them for an extra 3 plus percent ($10,000 on a $300,000 home). The NAR disagrees with these studies and points out that, generally, owners of lower-priced homes try to sell on their own. Most owners do not try to sell their own homes, and realtors continue to "own" the market, largely because of the prominence of the MLS and laws that support their place in the industry.

There are changes afoot – changes in metadata that may change the industry. **FranklyMLS**, a wiki-based approach to home listings, is taking root on the East Coast. It makes excellent use of satellite photos and other map data. Both realtors and homeowners are contributing, and the wiki approach seems to be working. **Redfin** and **ZipRealty** operate realtor-friendly services that use the realtor network but give generous rebates to buyers to reduce commissions; both these sites are growing. Sites like **Trulia**, **StreetEasy**, **Roost**, and **Zillow** have much more information on properties than the MLS sites do. StreetEasy told me its traffic had quadrupled in 2008 – a terrible year for real estate! Now that buyers look at so many different sites to research homes, **Dwellicious** lets you assemble a list of potential homes from many sites and updates the list in real time as the metadata changes.

The Power Shift

I have no problem with realtors – some of my favorite siblings are realtors. But I managed to find my home on Craigslist, and the owner-to-owner transaction was smooth and easy, not unsafe and scary. Yet many realtors work hard and provide a valuable service to both buyers and sellers who don't want to do it themselves. Will we see the opening of metadata markets and a shift in the NAR to embrace a twenty-first-century pull model? Will you keep your home description in your own data locker and then allow the NAR access to it if you decide to use a realtor? In short, will NAR embrace open standards and more choices for consumers, even if it means that the way realtors see their place in the market will have to change fundamentally?

Surprisingly, I think it will. After a long conversation with NAR senior vice president and chief technology officer Mark Lesswing, who oversees NAR's Center for Realtor Technology, I believe the industry is heading in the right direction. The problems Lesswing faces are worth exploring.

First, there are realtors – the accredited, licensed salespeople who represent both buyers and sellers. Go to Realtor.com and look at a listing for a home. When you look at an MLS listing, you are looking only at the most visible part of a complicated contract signed between seller and sales agent. It's actually an offer, in the same way that an eBay listing is an offer. If the information were syndicated somewhere and a mistake or false claim made its way into a listing, the listing agent could be held liable for damages. Not surprisingly, agents feel the need to have as much control over their listings as possible.

Second, there are islands of MLS listings. They have a single, common format, called the Real Estate Transaction Standard (RETS). They also have a saying: Real estate is local. Each local group has managed to make so many custom changes to its software that the standard is now a patchwork quilt of custom descriptions and locally written software. There has been a great degree of semantic dispersion, almost no shared vocabulary, no data portability, and strong reluctance to develop a common standard.

Feed Control

Should you control who can do what with your metadata? If it's private or subscription-based, you have to. But, as we've seen, in most industries, product descriptions are going to be free. If they are semantic and free, won't anything and everything happen to them? Will we see both orthodox metadata and progressive metadata living together on the very same page?

Buyers tend to look online for more information, like sales histories and lawsuits. They certainly want to know anything that might be bad for them, no matter where it comes from. Wouldn't you? Realtor.com (and its next incarnation, Move.com) is already losing market share to sites with much more information. And the semantic web is about making *everything* more findable. Companies like GoodGuide, Planet Feedback, and Consumer Reports exist because prospective buyers look for reviews and complaints about a company, a person, a home, or a product. The more you try to control the message, the more popular the investigative sites become.

Third, there are privacy issues. What if an enterprising programmer combines a broker's listing with a public database and points out that a convicted sex offender lives on the same block? What if the broker is responsible for making sure people don't see who's living in the home during the listing? What if there's a divorce involved and the owners want to keep it quiet? How can the broker sign a contract with a client and ensure his or her privacy if the information is going to be all over the open web?

Mark Lesswing and his group are trying to balance all these realtor issues with the needs of buyers, who seem to get more sophisticated daily. Like many industries, the NAR doesn't have an overall strategy for how it will syndicate metadata as the semantic web takes shape. It is making incremental changes, taking small steps to help reduce costs and add flexibility. It has a working group hammering out the next standard, RETS 1.5. Approving that standard could be the big step that puts real estate metadata on the path to pull.

Lesswing needs to do a small version of what Mark Bolgiano has done in financial reporting. He has to assemble the standards, the resources, and the political will to get everyone going in the same direction. If the NAR has people like Mark Lesswing and his team on board, someday real estate will make its way into the twenty-first century. Here are just a few of the possible scenarios:

Semantic search engines would find all the MLS listings and all the listings in all the data lockers (that people want to expose).

Mash-ups do interesting things with the data. Take a look at Housing maps.com, Rentometer.com, and Homethinking.com. There are plenty of creative people eager to pitch in and make real estate metadata more interesting and discoverable, if only they can get better data.

Listings become portable, so you can list your home on as many sites as you like. You only need to fill out one listing form and then syndicate it to any specialty sites you want.

Your personal data locker generates your listing automatically. Who needs a special web site when the property's description is already available in a semantic format via your data locker and the search engines can see that format on the open web? Indicate your selling price, add some nice words to make it sound good, and your data locker pulls the buyers in to you in seconds. In fact, your home is *always* for sale at *some* price. You never fill out a listing form, ever. You just adjust your price and wait for offers to come in.

Listings are free. On eBay, the price for listing a home for thirty days is currently $150. Putting a listing into an MLS today costs $400 and up. It requires a thick contract and a chain of responsibility. If people at Yahoo have their way, your listing will be online and visible for free.

The home management area of your data locker ties in to the entire process, working with title insurance, banks, lawyers, contractors, inspectors, and other service providers. Why pay for an appraisal when your property is always appraised? Your personal data locker becomes the information hub for working on your transaction. Service providers come to you, and the data stays in one place. Your data locker eliminates the need for services like LendingTree.com and many others that duplicate metadata and distribute it in exchange for a small slice of the pie.*

The line between realtors and owners blurs, as more owners choose to purchase services à la carte, rather than in one expensive package at a fixed rate. Anyone can help sell or buy a home and get paid market rates for the value she adds. There's nothing dangerous about this – the online transaction guides you through the process step by step, bringing in professionals as needed.

Realtors eventually change to performance pricing, where they negotiate their fees up front based on their track records and the value they provide. Now realtors compete against nonrealtors – people who are unlicensed! – on a level playing field. This goes for both residential and commercial realtors and listings.

---

*The Mortgage Industry Standards Maintenance Organization (MISMO) has created a new standard for loan applications for commercial and residential real estate, designed to operate in an open, transparent, vendor-neutral environment. It estimates that its standards will save the industry an average of $250 per loan. MISMO is a truly portable standard, the antidote to silos like LendingTree.com. See **MISMO.org**.

Hardworking realtors have nothing to fear from more and better market data. They will command the highest prices and be worth every penny of what they charge, while perhaps half a million realtors in the United States who add little or no value and act as gatekeepers will have to find more productive employment elsewhere.

Laws change. In California, it's practically impossible to sell a home without a realtor. There are too many liabilities and responsibilities – realtors are practically baked in to the legal system. While laws should protect buyers, sellers, and agents, they should not protect the monopoly realtors have on listings and commissions.

Looking for a home becomes a matter of specifying a "want" in your data locker and seeing a list of homes that match. According to the NAR, 87 percent of all homebuyers used the Internet to search for homes in 2008. Which would you prefer: to do keyword searches on several different web sites or to see 100 percent of the inventory available as a result of your semantic query? (See Chapter 10 for a description of semantic search.)

Realtors make changes to their contracts and accept the fact that their data is going to get out of their control. That's the honest approach, and it's also a good business strategy. In the end, trust will be a factor of transparency, not control. When people trust realtors to be on their side 100 percent, everyone will profit.

Like many other industries, this one gets almost no leverage from its data. Home searching and buying is a long, complicated, mostly manual process, presided over by people wielding outdated contracts, cottage-industry software, and stacks of paper forms filled out in triplicate. Consumers don't want to be locked in to this antiquated process – they want to take advantage of the reusability of their information and the flexibility of the semantic web to maximize their desires.

What is the realtor of the future? There will always be a need for smart, strategic marketing of homes. But our data lockers and software agents will take care of the transaction mechanics. Rather than holding on to their fixed commissions, I believe real estate agents will have to negotiate their commissions up front, the way lawyers and investment bankers do.

End of Life

Many years later, it's time for the next homeowner to replace the superefficient refrigerator with an even better model. What should we do when our appliances and homes are ready to make way for something new? The cradle-to-cradle movement started by architect William McDonough and Dr. Michael Braungart focuses on materials and design, using material in closed loops that go back where they came from or into another product at the end of life.

As the pull era emerges, we'll include semantic life-cycle information in this loop, providing feedback that not only helps us make and use products better but also helps us dispose of them. When products are no longer useful, we can help them find their next homes by letting online scavengers pull them apart virtually. If you're done with your old phone, you can make it available via your data locker and someone will offer to come pick it up (or you can just toss it in the mail with his i-name written on it). The locker-to-locker trading system works day and night to help you get what you want and get rid of what you don't want. This isn't just for consumers – companies will find the waste products that will become inputs to their processes. Today, they have no idea what might be nearby and useful. Tomorrow, they will use the power of the semantic web to close the loop, finding clever solutions to hard industrial problems.

Future Urban Planning

Back to the urban planning hall in Shanghai. The year is 2030. The scale model is gone. The building is now an art museum. The model of

Shanghai is now virtual and online. It's no longer a tourist destination, but it is tremendously useful, because each physical building sends in its data as it is built. Each building will broadcast its own data. The city model then aggregates and displays the information. Different people use it for all different purposes, from studying hydrology to planning a democracy demonstration. Urban planners will see which buildings are being built and where they are in construction. They can run the clock forward or change the season to check shadows, sight lines, temperature and wind patterns, air pressure, parking, traffic, air quality, or earthquake-safety issues. They can watch the metro trains respond to changes in pedestrian patterns. The model ties into the city's schedule of events and weather measurements hundreds of kilometers away. It's a dynamic tool that helps adjust the workings of the city in real time, responding to the needs of the minute, the hour, and the day. And it's constantly self-assembling from millions of sensors and data points reporting in.

Cities are made of buildings and the infrastructure to support them. The information in the data locker is a mirror of a building and its contents. When it's time to sell a home or an office tower, both buyers and sellers will have many more choices than they have today.

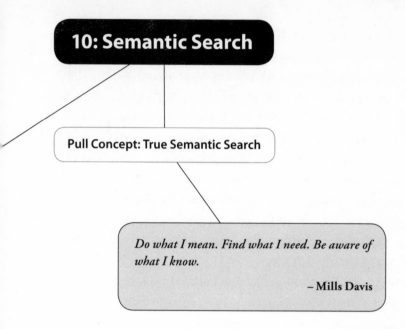

10: Semantic Search

Pull Concept: True Semantic Search

Do what I mean. Find what I need. Be aware of what I know.

– Mills Davis

THERE'S A GOOD REASON the search industry and the marketing industry are so closely linked – a search is a signal that someone is looking for something. That's half the marketing equation right there. The other half is the product, service, content, or *something* that someone has to offer. In this chapter, I'll show how semantic search will evolve to help connect people better to the things they are looking for and how that will affect advertising. In Chapter 11, we'll look at how marketing will change once we have all our information and preferences in our online data lockers.

The average knowledge worker spends 2.3 hours per day – about 25 percent of work time – searching for critical job information.[23] Americans now do about 7.5 billion searches on major search engines every month, and about *one-third* of all searches do not lead to a click.[24] People spend a lot of time trying to think of the right way to express what they are looking for. Google has learned, for example, that people have managed to spell "Britney Spears" at least 600 different ways.[25]

If one-third of searches don't lead to a click, I'm willing to bet another third lead to a dead end. If the average person searches, say, three times using three different search terms or clicks on several sites before finding what he or she is looking for, it's likely that around 90 percent of searches don't hit their target. Is this good for search engines?

Yes. Think about how search engines get paid. They don't get any money when you get what you want from your natural search results. They get paid when you *don't* get what you want from your search results, but you see something interesting above or on the side and click on that. The search engine cares that after you hit ENTER, the results page delivers clicks for advertisers, to the tune of about $40 billion globally each year.[26] That's what they are trying to maximize. Keep that in mind as we review the various aspects of online search.

Apples to Apples

The true goal in search is to give people exactly what they are looking for at once, in the context of their needs at that time. To be precise, we're looking for relevant search results that have no false positives and no false negatives. A **false positive** is when something shows up on a search that shouldn't be there. For example, I'm looking for a doctor to help me with my knee pain, so I go to Google and type in: "New York knee joint clinic." The first four results are for a knee and joint clinic in Houston that was written up in the *New York Times*. All the words are on that page, but what I'm looking for isn't. Another example: I'm looking for some wrist pads to stick to my laptop to help my wrists while writing this book. Some time ago, I went to Amazon.com and entered "stick on wrist pads," and here was the single result:

Sexual Segregation in Vertebrates,
by Kathreen Ruckstuhl and Peter Neuhaus; $106

I'm pretty sure that's a false positive. We see these kinds of results often, yet we tend not to think about how much time they waste. We just make changes to our keywords and try again.

A **false negative** is when something doesn't show up on a search that *should* be there. The worst example is if I'm looking for something – anything – and my neighbor or a business next door just happens to have one available, but I have no way to know that.

It's very difficult to make a thorough search that nets only the things you're interested in and none of the things you're not, and gives you a basis for comparing features with precision – especially when the majority of information is buried inside of databases and much of it is not exposed to search engines in the first place.

Can Google show you all the silver Porsche 996 Turbos built from 2000 to 2004 with black interior and fewer than 30,000 miles for sale within a thirty-minute drive of your home? Can it show them sorted by features, price, mileage, or service record? Can Bing tell you how many people work as cashiers in the United States? Can Yahoo show you which movies with monsters in them grossed over $100 million in the last five years? Can Google find you a business-class hotel in Tel Aviv with an event room for 185 people available for two days in March? Can About.com tell you where you left your sunglasses? Can Ask find you a great director of marketing?

No, and I'm not just picking on these specific search engines. Keyword-based search engines use many sophisticated tricks to index the web, but they can only point you to web pages, and those web pages may have had the information on them at one point, or they may have similar keywords on them, or they may have nothing of interest, or they may contain the exact answer you were looking for. It's up to you to look at those pages and decide for yourself.

In contrast, semantic search promises to be much more productive. In semantic search, you give a query and get an answer. If you are looking for something to buy, you specify your order and see the offers.

Ultimately, we want apples-to-apples comparisons of information, products, and services *webwide*, not just inside a particular database. Let's work our way there quickly.

Vertical Search

A mainstream search engine that has to help people find anything, anywhere, anytime must do a lot of guessing. But search engines that focus on specific areas can build more structure behind the scenes, so they can relate concepts within their domain for more accurate results.

Lightly structured data, like pages that describe doctors, real estate listings, consumer elecvtronics, books, movies, cars, restaurants, and wine, is relatively easy to collect and aggregate. There may not be a common format and the data may not be complete, but if you're only looking for wine descriptions and nothing else, you can usually figure out quite a bit. Your resulting list may not be perfect, but it will be useful. Several specialty search engines, like Zillow.com, Transparensee.com, and AdaptiveBlue.com, go after this low-hanging fruit by adding their own structure to bring you more relevant search results. This kind of specialized search is called vertical search. The success of several vertical-search startups demonstrates the demand for more accurate search results.

Text Analytics

Google has started to try to figure out what you mean when you type a query (rather than a keyword) into their search engine. Ask it, "What is the capital of Oregon?" and it will display a link to the city of Salem. Ask it, "Who is Bill Clinton's mother?" and it will display a link to a page on Virginia Clinton. It can't tell you who Francis Ford Coppola's ex-son-in-law is, which museums in New York are open on Monday, which after-market mufflers go on a 1972 Ford Mustang, or the size of the commercial real estate market in the United States, but it's a start. Google uses its own semantic system behind the scenes to scrape information from web sites and figure out what the relationships are.

This is the field of *text analytics:* taking unstructured information, like web pages, interviews, blogs, video clips, and news stories, and building a semantic structure behind the scenes using software to do the tagging automatically. Then it allows you to ask questions in plain English: for example, "On what date did Al Gore win the Nobel Prize?" The structured database behind the scenes will answer questions better than searching by keyword. Here are a few cutting-edge examples from today's pseudo-semantic web:

Financial: Newssift.com, from the *Financial Times,* searches 4,000 business-news sources and automatically tags over 100,000 stories a day, focusing on business relationships.

News: Zantaz.com provides semantic tools to many businesses. One application, called eDiscovery, helps financial institutions scan millions of email messages to answer questions from compliance officers on topics of interest. Doing this by hand or by keyword alone would be prohibitively expensive. **Daylife.com** scans the news space and puts together a user experience very different from other news outlets. There you can see structured "scorecards" on people, places, and companies. You can search photos by topic, look for quotes, and see a time line of any news topic.

Legal: Autonomy.com makes tools for searching large datasets. One of its projects, for Linklaters in London, helps this large law firm of 2,000 lawyers in thirty offices find conflicts of interest. By searching all their databases, with records of more than 250,000 companies and 100,000 transactions, they now perform over 100 automated conflict searches every day – something that would take a team of ten people or more.

General knowledge: The True Knowledge answer engine (TRUE KNOWLEDGE.COM) combines text analytics with a structured database of facts it has harvested from the web. It's quite good at giving straight answers to many common questions.

Health: Healthline.com searches the medical literature and has built the world's largest taxonomy of health terms (1.3 million plus) to make searches on its site more meaningful. The company has built thousands of HealthMaps that help show the relationships between terms. The system knows, for example, that the herpes simplex virus can cause pneumonia.

Structured Search

When searching for something, most people are usually comfortable with working their way toward it, adding information as they go. Once we have an answer, we want to ask:

What's above? What's this a part of?

What's below? What does it contain? What are the subcategories?

What's adjacent? What's related? How is it related?

To help narrow down results, a search engine must have a **concept model**, with categories, relationships, and meanings (definitions) of people, places, and things in the real world. In semantic search, we specify these explicitly up front. (More on that in a minute.) In structured search, the software assembles them from the symbols and text found on web pages, trying to infer the relationships and hoping to get it right most of the time.

Several new projects take just that approach, inferring structure from what's already on the web to return *a framework for answers* to queries, rather than a single answer or a list of web pages. The goal is to create context around the answer, helping the user refine or expand her request. These companies already employ thousands of people, hoping to cash in on the next frontier of the search business.

Google Squared is the Google approach to structured search. Type in a query and Google Squared gives a grid of what it thinks are the relevant categories of answers. The grid looks like a spreadsheet, with columns of attributes and rows of potential answers. For example, type in "California roller coasters," and Google Squared returns a list of roller coasters. For each one, it shows the name, location, age, a representative photo, total length, number of inversions, maximum speed, and special features. It even gives you a blank column, where you can type a keyword and it will try to fill in that column as best it can. Click on the heading for any column and the list re-sorts itself. For many searches, Google Squared will facilitate true apples-to-apples comparisons. For many others, the results will be nonsensical and meaningless, because the information is too difficult to determine without help.

WolframAlpha has a different approach. Like True Knowledge, it takes natural-language queries and tries to give exact answers, but it focuses more on current facts and figures. The company employs hundreds of "curators", who find the most authoritative sources for specific information and add the structure and tags necessary to make the relationships explicit. A search for "Paris, France" gives you a map, the population, the current temperature, and various facts and figures about Paris. Ask it "MSFT cash / MSFT shares" and it will tell you how much cash Microsoft has per share in several different currencies. Type in "international space station" and it will tell you where the space station is over Earth *right now*.

WolframAlpha is very oriented toward numbers, graphs, diagrams, and real time, and it lists the sources of its data. WolframAlpha has become a magnet for serious data providers, who can now publish information in Wolfram-native format. If the WolframAlpha internal formats evolve into open standards, this company could jump-start the semantic web singlehandedly.

Structured search is a transitional strategy toward true semantic search. WolframAlpha will return stunningly accurate results on a tiny subset of the entire web, while Google Squared will try to put something in each box, even if it's comically wrong. Google does more guessing but covers a much wider topic space.

Semantic Search

Yahoo gets credit for embracing many of the formats of the semantic web, giving at least some search results that are fully semantic from the start. Yahoo knows, for example, that if your résumé is in the hResume microformat, it's a résumé, no matter what site it is on. Someone looking for your online résumé should find it using Yahoo alone.

Yahoo has taken semantics a step further with its **SearchMonkey** program, and it deserves a deeper look. SearchMonkey gives site owners the ability to add structured information that the Yahoo search engine can see. You can even build your own applications to help the Yahoo search engine extract information from your site.

Microformats

A few people saw a need for simple, reusable building blocks of information, so they started a grassroots movement to create and govern them. Microformats are "designed for humans first and machines second," which means they can be written and read easily, like the first web sites. Many microformats start with a lowercase *h* – hCard, hResume, hCalendar, hRecipe, hReview, etc. Their goal is to extend the web with lightweight packets of semantic data as they are needed. They try to solve 80 percent of the problem quickly and not get bogged down trying to define the last 20 percent. Learn more at Microformats.org.

To imagine a fully semantic search, go to SeamlessWeb.com and explore the restaurants in your neighborhood. There's a stunning amount of semantic information on this site – each restaurant has its complete menu listed, including potential options, and all prices.

If you're a restaurant owner, you must go to the "rear entrance" of this site and enter all your information into the database. If you want to change a price, you must go back, log in, and change it. Furthermore, you need to do that for *all* sites with restaurant listings, which means you spend a lot of time entering and updating information on all the different sites.

Is it semantic? SeamlessWeb menus are extremely specific, and well structured, but the format is proprietary. Is it on the web? No. These sites are useful, but they are silos with no leverage. In the semantic web, a restaurant owner will put her menu on her *own* site in a common format and all the restaurant-ordering engines will come get it.

Go to Amazon or Blue Nile and you'll see sophisticated interactive tools for finding diamonds. You can move the sliders to show the ranges of diamond attributes. As you move them, you see all the results immediately. (I highly recommend trying it – the experience is very satisfying. See illustration next page)

The diamond finders at Blue Nile are extremely semantic (unambiguous), but they aren't part of the semantic web. In the semantic web, the description of *every diamond in the world* will be online. As you move the sliders on a global diamond finder, stones from every dealer in every country appear and disappear. You can filter by cut, clarity, color, weight, distance, shipping costs, fluorescence, table, girdle, angles, dealer reputation, etc.

Microformats, SearchMonkey, and WolframAlpha represent the beginning of fully semantic search. The big difference between structured search and semantic search is that semantic search works much more often. Rather than search engines guessing, the people with the information put it into a common format themselves and make it available online. For example, airlines will start publishing their route and schedule data in a format that all search engines can understand, while displaying human-readable information on their own web sites. A restaurant can put its own menu on its own site using a microformat, and

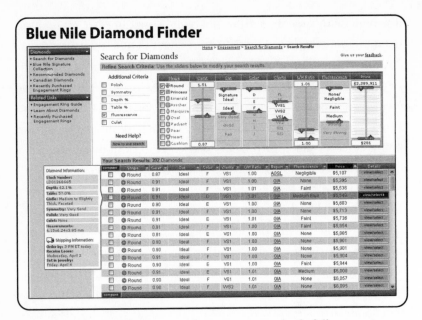

Blue Nile's diamond finder is unambiguous, an example of a fully semantic search.

now the search engines can hook you up with an ordering-and-delivery engine that lets you choose a restaurant and place your order. Clothing companies specify all their sizes, colors, and features using open formats, letting consumers compare a single kind of product among thousands of vendors. Corporate purchasers can compare offers directly.

That's the semantic web. It's not going to spring into existence overnight, but the seeds of the semantic web are already germinating and growing quickly. As we've seen, several of the standards for describing content semantically already exist, and more are coming every day. As people start to use them to describe their products and services, they will get more customers as a result of more accurate search results. Over time, it will change the way we all interact with information every day, and it will disrupt the search business entirely.

We'll start by combining it with text-based searches so that if our first try isn't perfect, we can turn a keyword search into a query and refine

the results semantically, getting closer and closer to what we are looking for. Text analytics will get us started, and semantic structure will
help us narrow down the choices quickly. Much of the time, we won't
even think about the difference between free-text search and semantic
search. We'll go back and forth, looking for answers rather than web
pages, typing in or asking by voice, using semantic queries without
even knowing that's what we're doing.*

What's Next

Companies that sell keywords today may not want to see their business
models crushed by the sledgehammer of the semantic web. They rely
on people bumping into sites by accident as they surf. They aren't sure
how to get ad revenues from the deep web or from searches that are too
accurate. They may avoid the semantic web not because they can't see it
coming but precisely because they *can* see it coming and can't monetize
it as effectively as the keyword-driven searches of today.

Several early readers of this book cursed me for making them con-
scious of how frustrating their searches really were. Will people learn to
search semantically? I think they will. They do at Blue Nile and CNET
every day. I expect Google Squared and WolframAlpha to be quite
popular by the time you read this. To pass the semantic-search acid test,
however, we'll have to see more data sources uploading data in common
formats to the open web. But you already knew that.

The basic unit of a semantic search is a query – a question a search engine
can understand without having to guess. Queries are to semantic search
what keywords are to today's search engines. When our data lockers ask
the questions for us and filter the answers according to our personal ontologies, perhaps the search of the future really will be – no search at all!

---

* A voice interface must figure out what you've said before it can figure out what you
mean. Try it using your iPhone at **Siri.com.**

11: Pull Marketing

Pull Concept: Account Portability

> *Pushing a message at a potential customer when it has not been requested and when the consumer is in the midst of something else on the net, will fail as a major revenue source for most Internet sites.*
>
> – Eric Clemons,
> **Wharton School of Business**

I KNOW PRETTY MUCH EVERYTHING there is to know about diabetes test kits and home scooters. Why? Because I watch CNN all day. CNN doesn't know I would be much more interested to learn about the latest powder skis and titanium strollers than the latest incontinence products or vacuum cleaners. Even when we buy keywords from search engines, we are still guessing. How many times have I seen an ad from Amazon.com asking me if I want to buy a book on oil changes or Japanese restaurants in San Francisco? One hundred percent of the time we watch TV – in fact, in one hundred percent of the advertising we see – marketers and advertisers are guessing that they know what we want. Ninety-nine percent of the time, they are wrong, and they know that, too. We're so used to guessing that we're unaware of any other way to do business.

Measurement and extrapolation are the science behind today's marketing. Companies use Nielsen ratings and web analytics to break customers into segments by demographics, psychographics, behavior, etc. The groups are big, they are fuzzy, and they mean practically nothing. We've heard about "markets of one" for years, but we haven't had the tools to make them a reality.

We never will. We'll never have the tools to do traditional push marketing to individuals. The only way to apply marketing to individuals is to let them pull on their end of the rope. The power shift of the semantic web will give all customers – whether individuals or institutions – the tools to do their own marketing in the other direction. This chapter is about changing from push marketing to pull marketing – giving our customers the chance to say what they are looking for and helping them find it – even if it's not in our best short-term interest to do so.

Vendor Relationship Management

At this moment, all car companies are investing heavily in the "online user experience," which they want to be a seamless, branded interaction between you, your car, and their marketing department. They want the experience to be "sticky," so you get emails about your car with links to your personal area on *their* web site.

That's push marketing, circa 1998, when all the business books espoused just that strategy. In the pull era, the relationship is reversed. In the world of pull, the vendor no longer owns the customer. A person with three cars doesn't want to log in to three different web sites to manage information and get the latest offers. As we've already seen, the person who owns a house isn't interested in logging in to dozens of web sites to see how the appliances are doing.

Managing customer-vendor metadata from the customer end is called Vendor Relationship Management (VRM), a term coined by Doc Searls at the Berkman Center for Internet and Society at Harvard University, where the project is based. The Berkman Center's aim is to reverse the typical Customer Relationship Management (CRM) tools from company-centered to customer-centered. It is starting with portable data standards that will eventually become part of your online data locker.

Vᴙм

What will vᴙм do to make surveys stop sucking? Two words: eliminate guesswork.
– Doc Searls

With vᴙм, you can participate in rewards programs and focus groups, receive discounts, and get product news by pulling them into your email account at first and your data locker later. You control the data that would normally be in a cʀм system, so you can give it to the next vendor in the same way vendors pass customer data from one sales rep to another. Using the principle of least privilege, you can give out your data as necessary and terminate the relationship at any time. When a product goes into the "haves" section of your data locker, the warranty record follows automatically. Without knowing your name and address, the company can contact you if there's a problem, and you can contact the company. You can signal that you are planning to switch vendors, and all vendors will come to you with their offers, knowing what you have and what kind of customer you are.

Account Portability

When you opened your bank account, you filled out a few pages of paperwork. Someone later rekeyed that information into the bank's database. How easy is it to move your account to another bank? It's easier to move your family to Kazakhstan. It won't start in banking, but eventually most companies and even the government will agree to **account portability**, because consumers will demand it. Once the banks agree to a portability framework, however, the game is over for the banks. You'll turn the situation around by transferring all your assets to your personal data locker, rather than another bank, and then you'll have the power in the relationship. With an online personal data locker, all your money, assets, and information will live in one single place, and you will be able to invite any bank you want to come manage any part or all of it.* If you loan money to a bank, the bank will put an IOU in your personal data locker. If you want to buy stocks, a registrar will link the virtual stock certificates to your data locker, so you can use any broker you like for each transaction.

First, we'll make data portable, then we'll port it to our data lockers, then we'll manage our information from there. This isn't some cool idea for a new start-up – it can be implemented by anyone anywhere, using publicly available standards for data portability. Once you have your information under your control, you'll become an **institution of one**, with more bargaining power and leverage than you ever had before. Learn more about all the new standards at **DataPortability.org.**

Semantic Marketing

I've described all these semantic innovations to bring us to the money point of this chapter: that semantic search and personal control of information will affect companies down to their core, right to their mission statements and corporate cultures. Most companies are in business to make money by focusing on their own needs, and that has served them well during the push years. But in the pull era, we change from a "seller-centric" business model to a "buyer-centric" point of view. As Alan Mitchell, a consultant in the UK, explains:

---

*This will require some changes to federal and state laws, but eventually you'll have a virtual lockbox from which to manage your own account.

Traditional seller-centric organizations are focused on improving the economics of the firm. Only if the firm improves its economics can it pass benefits back to customers in the form of better products and services and/or lower prices. So every issue, problem, and opportunity is addressed from this standpoint: does it – how can it – improve the economics of the firm?

Buyer-centricity turns this on its head. Its purpose is to improve the economics of the individual. If the economics of the individual improve, then that individual is in a position to pass some of the benefits back to his suppliers. This increased "investment" may take many forms – more money, time, information, attention, work, emotional engagement, whatever. But its value is unquestionable.

Marketing in this context is nothing short of total customer advocacy, even if that conflicts with the economics of the firm. We are entering an age of unparalleled transparency and honesty. We must start to respond to our customers' needs in real time, rather than try to get them to swallow the products and services we have on hand. The tactics may come and go, but pulling information requires a change of strategy.

A good example is the car web site I described earlier. The people at all the big car companies are spending millions to make sure your online interaction with their company goes through the web site that will come with your car. They don't really want to fit into the buyer's ecosystem, where critics are comparing and testing cars, giving honest opinions, and showing workaround solutions to problems. They don't want a single detractor of their products to have an adjacent voice. They don't want to have to put out a growing brushfire online if someone has a bad experience. And the last thing they want is for you to manage your car's data on your own terms, from your own data locker. As the metadata goes, so goes the relationship. Marketers will need to find a way to fit in or say good-bye to the account.

Advertising

Since advertising drives the online search industry, to the tune of $40 billion per year globally, it seems appropriate to build a semantic-advertising BS detector, so we can see what's going to be disruptive and what makes for a good press release. Advertising will continue to be part of the search experience, and it will continue to influence search results. As search becomes more semantic, people will start applying their personal and corporate ontologies to their searches, and as the mass market shrinks, a new era of advertising will emerge. In a word, it will be *helpful*.

Consumers will pull advertising through willingly because it *enhances* their experience. Consumers will give advertisers access to their wants, needs, calendar, friends, and tastes. And they will expect a lot in return. If consumers with online data lockers could talk and advertisers could listen, this is what they would say:

> **You pay for all the content and web sites I want to experience.** Streaming music will be like having my own private mind-reading DJ. I'll listen to ads if they are relevant and fun. I'll pay for about 10 percent of my content and accept me-driven advertising on the other 90 percent.

> **I will rate the ads I see.** If I like your ad, I'll tell you that. If I don't like your ad, I'll tell you that, too. And I'll expect my feedback to make both of us happier in the long run.

> **At any given moment, I'm looking for something.** Help me find that something. Engage me. Entertain me. Look at my

calendar and see what's coming up. But don't show me prenatal vitamins or incontinence products unless you know I'm pregnant or spending too much time in the bathroom.* Don't cure me of anything I don't have. Bring me what I'm looking for, and I'll want more advertising in the future. I actually like ads that don't suck, so don't let them suck.

I'll data mine myself, thank you very much. I'm collecting data about and for myself that would be any marketer's dream. And I will give or sell my own information to advertisers if the deal is right. I'll control who can use this information and for what purposes. You can expect me to understand the principle of least privilege.

Know my context. Know my past, my experience, where I've been, what I've done. Pay attention to what I tell you and don't tell you. I may allow you to know what's in my closet or where I went on vacation. Know when I'm looking for baseball tickets for my nephew, when I'm looking for a summer camp for my son, and when I'm shopping for myself. Don't guess – know.

Earn my trust. If the thing I'm looking for isn't out there, don't show me a poor substitute. Show me a good substitute, based on my values. Impress me. Help me keep my commitments. Make it count.

Emotion still sells. But you have to reach me and my emotions, not what you *think* you know about me. I may be a member of several very different groups – don't assume I'm in the middle of those groups. I'm in each group individually for different reasons with different goals.

---

* I specifically do *not* predict that your toilet will recognize you and, well, let's say interact with your online data locker in a meaningful way. But in Japan I won't be surprised to see a wireless toilet within ten years.

Know what I like and how I like it. My calendar can tell you when I'm busy. My ontology can tell you what I like and how I like it. If we can navigate the delicate balance between leaning forward and leaning back, giving you what you want while getting what I want, we'll both benefit. Some days are not your day. Be patient.

Empower my friends to help reach me. I trust my friends. I often trust their taste in products and services. I often want their opinion on what I should buy. If you give my friend a discount on something, give her the ability to offer that discount to me. I'd much rather get it from her than from from you.

When you don't know, ask. That's right. Just ask. If you pay for my movies, news, shows, sites, and music, then I need you to tell me what you want. Feel free to be my partner.

The Power Shift

A search is a sign that someone wants something, which is why selling keywords has been profitable. In the pull era, a query is the start of a semantic conversation. It means a person is looking for offers.

There are many types of queries. Someone may have just changed her job status from "happily employed" to "willing to be taken to lunch." She may be looking for a new sofa that fits her living room, or she may need a home defibrillator by 4:00 P.M. today. Most semantic queries will specify a range; anything that falls within the range is a potential fit. For example, a bicyclist could be looking for shorts in his size, with pockets, in a certain price range. In that case, he wants to see exact matches. Other times, the criteria may be very flexible – we may not even know exactly what we are looking for.

The customer's data locker will be the gatekeeper. When we are pulling, the data locker will give you an opportunity to start a conversation, and your initial response will have to be 100 percent semantic. The data locker doesn't respond to sexy images and funny mascots. Only after your offer is inside the data locker will you have a chance to interact with its owner.

Imagine that you're working late with your regular crew and you get hungry. You interact with your data locker using your phone, headset, display – whatever device happens to be handy. Here's how the conversation might go:

You: Food.

Data Locker: Work dinner for four?

You: Yes.

That's it. Your data locker knows who is in the room. It has access to your coworkers' data lockers (to the extent needed for ordering dinner). It knows what kind of food you all like, and any aversions, allergies, or other requirements. It knows you're still at the office. It knows what time it is. It knows you all had Chinese food last night. It knows how adventurous you are in your tastes. And it can see the entire world of nearby vendors, semantic reviews, and product descriptions. Thirty minutes later, three different pizzas you all like (plus one salad, three Cokes, and one Diet Pepsi) show up at your door and the driver has already been tipped. You never asked for pizza, you just told your data locker you were hungry. And if the pizza hits the spot, you tell your data locker it was a great choice. If it doesn't, you each tell it what you didn't like, and it makes better choices next time.

Where is the vendor in this scenario? Where is the marketing message? Where are the logos and the taglines? Where is the music? Where's the brand loyalty? The stickiness? The conversation? If your information is sitting online as text, figures, animations, and PDF documents, as it is today, you will be invisible, irrelevant, out of the running. To be relevant, you have to be in the arena, and the arena, more and more, will be the performance arena.

And that, right there, is the tipping point. When you can just tell your phone you're hungry and delicious food at a price you want to pay shows up half an hour later, imagine how ordering supplies for your business is going to go. Imagine how people will choose cars, vacations, or contractors. Imagine how irrelevant today's marketing practices are in this economy. I don't think it takes too much imagination – it's just a matter of when, not if.

To summarize the world of pull marketing: all the customer data will soon belong to the customer. Whether it is a personal ontology for tastes and preferences, a body scan, a personal health record, a record of stock trades, or a purchasing history, customers will collect their own information and turn the tables on marketers. The pull power shift puts customers in charge. Companies that follow behind closest will come out ahead in the long run.

Risks and Creepiness

Does all this bring back memories of HAL, the computer in Stanley Kubrick's *2001: A Space Odyssey*? Does it sound like artificial intelligence will take over our lives and we'll find ourselves at the mercy of cyborg armies? It may not be that dramatic, but some people have concerns about everything I've described so far, and I want to address them here, in this chapter on marketing, where perception is often more important than reality.

Isn't having all our eggs in one basket a security risk? Different people have different views on this. Some people like having a separate key for every lock. They like the fact that it's difficult to replace keys, and if someone gets all your information in one silo, it's just a small part of everything you own. My response to this is: If someone had the single password to your bank account, couldn't he or she find a way to get most of your money out? How often have you heard about someone losing all her money to cyber theft, even though most of her money is in a single account? Not very often.

According to a Microsoft report, the average web user has twenty-five different password-based accounts. I believe that putting everything into a single data locker will be more secure, not less. Keep in mind that you'll have layers of privacy in your data locker, and you can put as many passwords and restrictions as you like on each one. You'll control who sees what, and you'll restrict anyone's access anytime you like.

What if the personal ontology gets out of control? What if there's a virus or a big company wants to influence it, or something we haven't thought about? What if someone working at your data locker company decides to leak your personal health information – couldn't that do irreparable harm? More realistically, what if you give your ontology to a marketer and then the marketer sells your data to everyone willing to pay for it, without your permission?

Valid concerns. You'll want to be anonymous more often than not, so you can interact with companies and give them information but not your identity. We will probably never know which link is the weakest in our online metadata chain. That's why I recommend being very careful when choosing a data locker provider. Though the standards may be universal, the level of security may not. The world will continue to be complicated and people will be taken advantage of, just as they are today. Those of us who watch for the conflicts of interest will likely have a safer experience than we do today, where conflicts of interest are involved in most of our online relationships. I like Facebook, but I'm not ready to store my personal medical history there. I'd rather pay more and get more. Get me to join for free, then charge me for premium services.

Could i-cards be another point of vulnerability? Many of the brightest people in the online security industry are working on i-cards. One thing they will do is eliminate **phishing** – the practice of luring people to phony web sites to get them to give out sensitive information. According to Gartner, phishing scams in 2007 convinced over 3.6 million Americans to hand over their credentials to a phony site, and they lost more than $3.2 billion. Serious, industrial-strength security will be behind many corporate and personal i-cards, making us safer than we are today. Companies like Microsoft, Novell, Google, and the Burton Group have excellent identity and security blogs that I believe will instill more confidence than terror in the new security schemes.*

If the online world mirrors the real world, aren't there predators and parasites who will take advantage of that? They already are, and they already cause us a lot of problems. Are you aware that your web-browsing history is being sold to marketers right now? I believe that going to new, semantically enabled security schemes will help us detect and deter them more effectively than we do today. This is a conversation worth continuing, but not here. I'll track this issue explicitly at **ThePowerofPull.com.**

What about Big Brother scenarios? It's disconcerting that the U.S. government has already used the Patriot Act to demand people's private web search histories, and that every message you send to a friend in China is monitored by Chinese officials. I believe we're more protected using the principles and tools I describe here. In the world of pull, we use government-issued i-cards only to deal with the government: paying taxes, voting, paying fines, crossing borders, using government services, and so on. Wouldn't you rather keep all your government forms online in your online data locker than where they are now?

So far, cybercrime has been big business and easy money without the semantic web. The technologies and practices I describe in this book will undoubtedly receive a response from those who want to steal from us and do harm to us. Yet they will have to do it on a new level, one that many web security experts believe will be more secure and harder to crack. In the coming years we'll see much less of the old-school tricks and perhaps a bit more of the serious kind of crime. The good news is that fewer criminals are easier to catch and put away because they are going after bigger prizes. The average web user should be much safer.

---

* See: IDENTITYBLOG.BURTONGROUP.COM, SRMSBLOG.BURTONGROUP.COM, IDENTITYBLOG .COM, and GOOGLEONLINESECURITY.BLOGSPOT.COM.

E-stonia

Estonia, a country of 1.35 million people just an hour's boat ride south of Finland, has 54 percent Internet usage but does 72 percent of its banking online and has mobile penetration of about 90 percent. Estonia's national e-ID card has the largest penetration of any such program in Europe, with about 1 million digital ID cards in the hands of Estonians. Each ID card has a chip, a photo, a government-issued email address, and a digital certificate for electronic signatures. Since 2005, Estonians' ID cards are the basis for their driver's licenses, mobile phone accounts, tickets on trains and buses, and other interactions with the government. Estonians pay for their parking meters by swiping their driver's licenses and walking away. By law, Estonians now pay taxes, vote online, and sign documents with their electronic IDs. The cards are so popular that many private banks and companies now accept them.

What's Next

As Peter Morville, author of *Ambient Findability*, says, "Findability is at the center of a quiet revolution." In this world, if you're not findable, you're not relevant. Staying relevant will be a huge priority for marketers as we move through the pull era and into the performance economy (see Chapter 16). Just to be found – just to stay in the game at all – you'll have to make your descriptions semantic. But to be *relevant*, you'll have to make a difference in people's lives.

Although we've already embraced several half in/half out strategies, we're starting to see the fully semantic approach establish roots. More and more marketers are making their way to SearchMonkey and building two-way communication into their products. Informed consumers are about to challenge marketers in new ways. People have problems. They want solutions. People have questions. They want answers. The messages of the past have almost nothing in common with the offers, counteroffers, and semantic market conversations of the future. Our data lockers will be at the center of those conversations. In Chapter 12, we'll see how we're about to make our data lockers much smarter.

12: The Knowledge Crisis

Pull Concept: Agility

> *The only way to rectify our reasonings is to make them as tangible as those of the Mathematicians, so that we can find our error at a glance, and when there are disputes among persons, we can simply say: Let us calculate without further ado, to see who is right.*
>
> **– Gottfried Leibniz, 1685**

WIKIPEDIA'S MORE THAN 2 MILLION ARTICLES are in free text format, with a few guidelines and common customs to make articles consistent for readers. In a lightly structured knowledge repository like Wikipedia, you make your way to a page, then you read the page to get the information. You can't get any more information out than the people who wrote the page put in.

If, instead of typing text, Wikipedians would do four things . . .

1. Enter their data as linked data using standard tags rather than just figures in text and tables,

2. Make factual statements using formal assertions with controlled vocabularies rather than free text,

3. Add a subject backbone and thesaurus to connect related terms together, and

4. Add a natural-language query processor

. . . then the WikiTextPedia could become WikiKnowledgePedia. It could answer hard questions written in English, like:

Which cities in the world have populations over 10 million?

Which museums in Paris are open on Mondays?

Is there a direct scheduled flight from Windhoek to Lusaka?

How big is the world economy?

Which John Wayne movies were made during the Vietnam War?

Which countries are the top consumers of chocolate, per capita?

How much do Americans spend on shipping every year?

What are the side effects of taking a certain three drugs at the same time?

Today on Wikipedia, if you want to see a list of cities sorted by population or crime rates, you must find a page where someone has entered that information by hand and others have kept it up to date. You can't work with, rearrange, or combine the data with other data. But in a WikiKnowledgePedia, those lists self-assemble on request from tagged data linked together in the model. It would find patterns, draw conclusions, and give answers that no single Wikipedia contributor knows.

A WikiKnowledgePedia like this would be a living, connected knowledge model. If you build a knowledge model in a careful, consistent way, you can use a **reasoner** to draw conclusions and make connections. Ask it: "Is Lampedusa part of Italy?" and the answer will come back: "Yes."

Ask it: "Is Tibet part of China?" and the answer will come back: "That's disputed." Ask it: "Which country most recently changed its government?" and you will get a different answer practically every week.

Once we have those standard tags and tools for making assertions inside Wikipedia, we can apply that same semantic tagging scheme to your company's intranet or to the entire web itself. As we add more information, the model gets smarter. This is important – if volunteers work hard to make a semantic version of Wikipedia, just connect that model to your intranet and *your intranet* will get much smarter very quickly. In fact, we can apply it to the entire web, tying the data formats and assertions together, and then the search engines will start answering real questions the way a human would.*

The sticking point, of course, is step number two, above. As you can probably imagine, getting people to enter assertions using formal logic statements is much harder than asking them to write in English. Someday, we'll have tools to help us do that. In the meantime, several groups have already taken Wikipedia's content and applied text analytics to extract the assertions and build a knowledge model. These efforts aren't useful yet, but they are interesting and will certainly get better. One is **DBpedia**, already part of the semantic web. It is an ontology with over 2 million working terms and 200 million assertions, many of them based on Wikipedia. (You can see more of these Wikipedia-based efforts at **Freebase.com** and **Semantic-MediaWiki.org.**)

What Is an Ontology?

An ontology is an **explicit knowledge model**. It's a formal way to declare the names of people, places, and things, along with their de-

---

* Some people take this one step further, saying that the web itself will become "sentient" and will be capable of reasoning on its own. This is called the "cognitive singularity."

scriptions, properties, and relationships, however complicated those relationships may be. We can use an ontology to categorize and describe a particular world flexibly, as in the GoodRelations product ontology. But we more often use an ontology to encapsulate what we know about a complicated subject space. Ontologies mirror the complex relationships we find in real-world systems, like the human body, a company, a disease, or the film industry.

What does an ontology look like? An ontology is a collection of "triples," each of which names two terms from the vocabulary and the relationship between them.

Wine Ontology Triples

winery	produces	wine
Rosenblum	is a	grape
zinfandel	tastes like	berry
zinfandel	is a	varietal
grape	is part of	wine
cabernet franc	is a	varietal
Francis Ford Coppola	is the father of	Sofia Coppola
Rosenblum	makes	zinfandel
winemaker	is part of	winery
Francis Ford Coppola	is a	winemaker
winemaker	makes	wine
zinfandel	tastes like	spice

Each row, or triple, of an ontology is called an assertion. The more true assertions you add to an ontology, the smarter it gets. Order doesn't matter – it's the aggregate knowledge encapsulated in all the assertions together that builds a knowledge model. We try to restrict the verb phrases in the middle to the fewest number possible. Adding new subjects and predicates on either side enriches the knowledge base.

Ontologies let us ask questions and see patterns in the data. We could take all the tasting notes from a site like Snooth.com and build an ontology from all the content on the site. Now we can ask:

> Which Napa Valley cabernets that retail for less than $30 taste of cherry, blackberry, and oak?
>
> Which wines taste similar to the winner of the grand prize of last weekend's virtual tasting and cost less than half the price?
>
> Which syrahs go well with smoked turkey?
>
> Which zinfandels are most consistent from year to year?

Ontologies help us model a process or a knowledge domain, even if the model has a lot of fuzzy concepts. This is how the human mind works, how we naturally forage for information, and how adaptive systems help us keep up with changes in the real world.*

Ontologies do what taxonomies can't – express complicated, convoluted, evolving relationships. And ontologies can hook to other ontologies. We can already see how this one might connect to a film

---

* In previous chapters, we've seen taxonomies as resources to encapsulate terms, definitions, even rules. Ontologies are much more capable, but they are different things to different people. They have their own problems as well as advantages. I'm not interested in the technical details or terms. In fact, I'm going to use the word "ontology" here to mean any flexible knowledge model that keeps adapting and learning as you add more information to it.

ontology. Using an ontology, a manufacturer can specify all the various components and options that go with its products. A chef can express the complicated relationships involved in baking a soufflé for one to one thousand people. A traveler can look at all the possible combinations of flights and trains to get from one place to another. Ontologies are flexible. Many parties can contribute to and share them, improving the model and its ability to answer questions.

We are already using ontologies to merge many large databases of knowledge. The protein ontology includes many protein databases and can be used to mine millions of assertions just by asking questions. It was built using standards for biological ontologies, so eventually it can be used in conjunction with gene ontologies and other knowledge bases. (Learn more at **ProteinOntology.org.au.**)

InSTEDD, an innovation lab for early detection and rapid response to disasters worldwide, uses ontologies to help make sense of event-based alerts as they come in from around the world. When there's a flu outbreak or a natural disaster, thousands of messages in many languages quickly make tracking the event an enormous task. Using ontologies prepared in advance, InSTEDD can decode all the messages and see patterns as the event unfolds.

An ontology doesn't have rules. It has assertions, and the assertions create patterns. New assertions can change the meaning of the entire ontology. As David Weinberger says:

> Something can be 78 percent in one pile, 63 percent in a second, and 54 percent in a third. . . . In the sort-of kind-of world, the percentages don't even have to add up to one hundred.

This book has a fixed taxonomy, which you can find at the table of contents. But the ideas in the book could really be expressed in many different arrangements and orders. I've had to choose a single taxonomy, but I'm sure there are many readers who could benefit from a different way of presenting the same information. Underlying all the

Pull Book Ontology

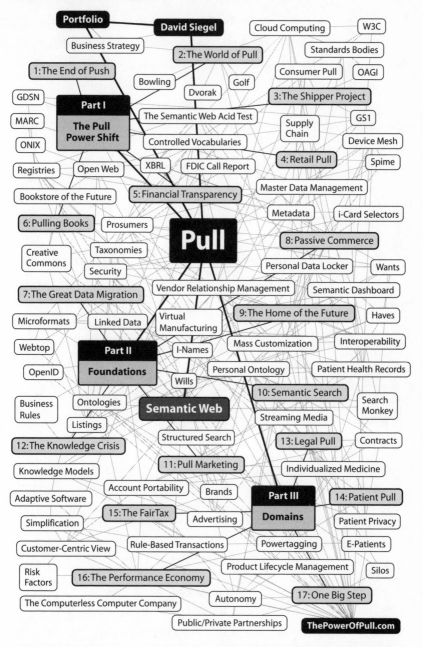

A bird's-eye view of the ontology of the concepts and terms in this book. Each line represents an assertion – a statement you could make about the two entities involved. Most of the lines represent "belongs to," "uses," or "works with" relationships. Conversely, where there are no lines there are no direct relationships.

possible different presentations is the **concept map**, which is exactly the kind of thing ontologies model. In this diagram, you can see both the hierarchy of the chapters and the underlying complexity of the interrelated concepts.

Just as molecular scientists build 3-D models to see molecular structure, ontologists use visualization tools to understand ontologies. I would love to present a gallery of cool ontology diagrams here, but I don't have space. You'll find it at **ThePowerofPull.com**.

Ontologies at Work

Ontology pioneers are already on the learning curve. Many thousands of ontologies have been built, some with more than a billion assertions. Very few of these projects justify their costs, but the next generation should have a more viable business case. While most ontologies are research projects, the following ontologies are hard at work saving money and time, and teaching their designers how to work with flexible knowledge models:

NASA has built an organization-wide "expert finder" that helps people find who knows what in the organization.

Eli Lily uses a huge ontology of research findings to explore for promising drugs to match against business requirements.

Procter & Gamble is using semantic agent technology for supply chain inventory optimization.

Renault uses linked data and an ontology to model the complicated relationships between components, parts, problems, diagnostic tests, and failure rates. It solves hard diagnostic problems using a reasoner that takes many factors into account.

Southwest Airlines uses semantic technologies for network routing and scheduling optimization. The solution features agent-based modeling, aircraft autonomy, simulation of routing decisions, and adaptive scheduling and routing.

Audi uses a "virtual car" design environment that lets designers experiment with all kinds of new configurations of parts and features. An ontology represents the logic that coordinates all the functions, helping designers test and refine the interactions long before actually putting any parts together.

Boeing uses a thesaurus and ontology to help people find parts and experts if they only have a small piece of the puzzle and need to learn what's related or known.

The European Commission has dozens of ontology-based research projects aimed at making the business environment more productive. One, called APOSDLE, watches people working on their computers. In a separate window, it makes suggestions for documents, experts, and training modules that might be relevant to what they are doing.

Agfa built an ontology-based system of clinical guidelines and referral criteria for various kinds of diagnostic imaging. In the future, this could be used with electronic patient records as part of an expert system that assists doctors in decision making.

There are hundreds of ontology projects both in engineering and in research, especially in genetics and biology. They may not be right for your company yet, but it's worth following the developments in this space.

Business Rules

A big trend in enterprise software of the future will be to encode your business rules as a "cassette" of assertions that slides into your system and runs it. This modular approach uses ontologies to make the software more adaptive. Companies like ILOG build automated tools that help sketch, refine, and publish business rules that can go into various software systems. Companies at the cutting edge are already using flexible ontologies of business rules to improve loan processing, claims processing, hospital administration, financial decision making, and many other processes.

This "glass-box" approach to business rules eliminates big programming projects, software maintenance, and IT control over the process. It lets businesses become much more agile. As the organization learns, the system learns and can react faster and faster. Eventually, processes will change in real time, in response to business conditions.

Glass Boxes

Declarative systems allow applications that can learn, evolve, and use knowledge in ways the system designer could not foresee. A declarative representation is like a glass box with knowledge visible in a format that can be accessed, manipulated, decomposed, analyzed, and added to by independent reasoners. A procedural representation is like a black box with knowledge fixed and locked inside. Determined by algorithms, procedural systems do the same thing every time and cannot learn from experience.

– Mills Davis

Do the processes follow the rules? That's a question that today requires human interpretation (and plenty of consultants). In the pull era, the rules will change automatically in response to new information. We'll use ontology-based reasoning software to help us validate our processes, even as they change. The standard format is called the **Semantics of Business Vocabulary and Business Rules (SBVR)**. This and other standards will help us build a new generation of flexible, adaptive software that allows us to change both processes and rules as we go. Sounds technical, and it is.* A few forward-looking people are just now building the first scalable tools of the twenty-first century. As pulling information becomes more popular, their work will pay off.

Business Intelligence

Allow me to cut and paste the definition of business intelligence from Wikipedia, because it's so stunningly succinct:

> Business intelligence (BI) refers to skills, technologies, applications and practices used to help a business acquire a better understanding of its commercial context. Business intelligence may also refer to the collected information itself.

What do we mean by *semantic* business intelligence? Today, businesses gather data from many sources, and most of it doesn't pass our semantic web acid test. The goal of today's research and development on semantic web tools is to connect the dots and make information (and, therefore, insight) more discoverable amid the oversupply of business data.

That's fine. It's useful and it should be done. But I suggest that we are still guessing. I think we should be hooking our business intelligence systems to the semantic exhaust of our customers and prospective customers. I think we should be looking for those customers who are our biggest promoters, not by conducting surveys but by adding to our products and services the tools by which customers can tag their way into our strategic decision systems. Just as doctors will steer their decisions based on real feedback from real patients (see "power tagging," Chapter 14), there's no reason you can't ask customers ques-

---

*If you're frustrated I haven't gone further in this section, then **BusinessRulesGroup .org** is the web site you've been looking for.

tions directly and get real answers. Products could be messaging back to home base constantly, using a controlled vocabulary, giving direct feedback on their use, building a real-time dashboard of what's going on in the world right on your desktop.

I would go one step further and say that companies should be constantly promoting their promoters. Bring them into the process of planning and testing new products. We prosumers will be happy to let our favorite companies into our semantic data lockers and help them plan their next generation of products. And if there's a T-shirt involved, we'll be happy to give you our size. By working with real customers rather than pollsters, companies can innovate better and faster, and they'll have an instant rollout plan for bringing new, collaboratively planned products to market.

Knowledge Management

I'm not sure if we've spent more money building knowledge management systems that don't work or studying and reporting that they don't work. In today's knowledge management systems, everyone in a company is encouraged to add information to a separate repository and help others learn what they know. The problem isn't the software, it's the incentive. Who has time to maintain a bunch of metadata about a project, when the project takes sixty hours a week and the next one is already on your desk?

When we pull, rather than push, knowledge, we turn the model around, to what Ross Mayfield, CEO of SocialText, calls **manage knowledgement**:

> Manage knowledgement is a way of describing knowledge management that's backwards but works. With knowledge management, users were supposed to fill out forms as a side activity to extract their knowledge. Then some form of artificial

intelligence would extract value. Turns out, users resisted and the algorithms didn't match reality. With manage knowledgement, through blogs and wikis, the principle activity is *sharing*, driven by social incentives. Contribution is simple and unstructured, isn't a side activity, and there is permission to participate.

A semantic wiki-like approach is **Twine**, from Radar Networks. Twine helps individuals and groups organize, share, and discover information related to their interests. You can treat Twine like a wiki and enter everything about a project, from documents to messages to presentations and images. People can leave messages, organize subgroups, and link to resources inside and outside the company. With Twine, you tag as you go, adding structure while getting your work done.

The cool part: Twine *automatically* builds ontologies and vocabularies for you behind the scenes. It gives you topics you can search on and organize by. It lets you discover patterns and relationships that are not readily apparent. As you add documents and send messages, Twine builds a semantic model dynamically. And it can hook up to other Twines working on other projects. The company's philosophy is that you never touch the semantic mechanics – you just keep shoveling information in and let Twine do the sorting.

Wikis are powerful but unstructured tools. The future of knowledge management is to combine free-text systems people will use with more structured tagging that supports building ontologies. One way is to migrate information from our wikis into more structured tools as it becomes relevant – what Mayfield calls "making paths into roads."

The Semantic Dashboard

Once we have online data lockers, we'll need a new way to work with all our semantically enabled tools and content. Welcome to the semantic dashboard, which will appear on our device mesh and replace the Windows and Mac desktops we use every day.

The dashboard of the future won't recreate your familiar desktop in a browser window. It won't look like a suite of heavy applications. Today's "collaborative workspaces" are nothing more than online filing cabinets for the familiar documents and folder hierarchies of yesteryear.

Your online data locker will be project- or topic-oriented. It will give you a work environment for collaborating with hundreds of people and businesses. If you're designing a new drug, all the relevant tools for testing, research, nomenclature, marketing requirements, rules, and regulations will be in one place. If you are writing a novel, your dashboard will let you construct an environment that brings together your personal spellchecker, thesaurus, search results, character-development software, reference works, stylebook, plot software, collaboration wikis, etc. If you're designing a car or a building, just start a new facet in your dashboard and invite all the different collaborators to enter an environment semantically built for designing cars.

The days of general-purpose word processors and spreadsheets are over. Whether it's an itinerary, a menu, an expense report, an insurance form, an invitation, an application to a university, a grant application, or any other form, you'll fill it out using the format as a template to produce that document (similar to the tools that build the FDIC call reports I mentioned in Chapter 5).

When you apply to a university, your semantic dashboard will use the **common application** that over 300 universities now recognize (see **CommonApp.org**). Since your semantic dashboard already contains all your personal information (name and address, school report cards, etc.), the document will partially assemble itself and ask you questions for the rest.

We often don't adopt wikis and other online tools as readily as we should, because we spend much of our day in our email interface. Why take time to log in to a wiki, when I can just send a message instead? Then the messages proliferate and the project information scatters. In contrast, the semantic dashboard combines everything on one facet per project, so your email messages, wikis, groups, conversations, and documents for each project are all within easy reach. Each facet has its own messages and tools.

Perhaps the most exciting pilot project in this area is **Networked Environment for Personal Ontology-based Management of Unified Knowledge (NEPOMUK)**. It's bold, it's exciting, it's idealistic, and it's real. Funded with €11.5 million from companies like IBM, HP, SAP, and others, NEPOMUK has a chance to become the basis for online collaboration environments of the future. Its approach is to enable semantic wikis and tools that will eventually snap together to form modular smart systems.

The semantic dashboard will drive all the displays in your device mesh, from wrist- and pocket-size displays to walls and ambient systems that give us a much more immersive experience than we have today. Even now, you'll find you are much more productive using two displays than one.* I've described the office of the future a bit, and any science-fiction book can give you more detail. What makes all this possible is the adoption of the principles in this book. As the semantic web comes together, there will be a race to build the online data locker, and from that our semantic dashboards will emerge.

I can't tell you which company will bring us the true online semantic dashboard, but that's the ultimate platform of the twenty-first century. Could it be Mac.com? Mozilla.org? Google or Yahoo? A start-up? One thing's for sure: it will be connected, adaptive, intuitive, and integrated. It will look more like your phone than your desktop. At its heart will be your various ontologies, powering software agents to work on your behalf. Modules will plug in on demand. Everything will come and go as needed. Your health data, for example, could be scattered across the web, but it will appear as though it were right next to everything else.

---

*Learn more about using two screens to increase your productivity by searching online for **Randy Pausch last lecture**.

Personally, I'm hoping a new start-up will emerge and build a trusted brand that takes us all into a new era of personal productivity. If you want to help me start that company, or you're already working on it, please contact me.

The Work Ontology

I've mentioned the personal ontology often enough that you should now have a pretty good idea what it is. It specifies all your complicated tastes, requirements, constraints, beliefs, and desires as it learns about you by watching you go about your day. Because people wear many different hats, you'll build several ontologies. You'll have one for all your different roles – as a worker, a volunteer, a parent, a skydiver, etc. You'll probably share ontologies with various groups of coworkers. Your semantic dashboard has different contexts, so as you enter each facet of your dashboard, it knows which ontology to use.

Suppose you own a factory that makes concrete bricks. If your company's ontology knows about all the assets and processes, then you can play what-if using the ontology as a modeling tool. You can say, "What would it take to add another production line versus building a separate plant in another location?" and it will automatically go online, hook up to several brick-making ontologies, look up transportation costs from current tables, bring in the costing and estimating applications, search for everything necessary, cost out the machinery, installation, and additions to your infrastructure, and show you various scenarios. You'll make changes to the overall picture by saying you want more bricks per hour, you have clients farther away, you want larger production runs, or you need to start making more cinder blocks. The ontology will handle all the details, from sourcing components to costing out custom molds to estimating how much space you'll need for curing and storage, etc. In the spirit of the semantic web, you'll get work done by asking questions rather than assembling parts by hand.

Once the infrastructure is in place, your personal ontology combined with your semantic dashboard will be your "personal assistant" both at work and at play. Eventually, our semantic dashboards will do almost all of our administrative tasks, making us much more productive.

Web-Scale Ontologies

And now for a bit of extreme library science that may well become an important resource to your company. The **Large Knowledge Collider** (**LarKC**) is a project to do machine reasoning at a scale far beyond anything previously conceived. The goal is to harness thousands of computers across the web to process ontologies with *billions* of assertions. The founders call it a platform for semantic computing at web scale. They realize that for huge projects you can never have all the information or a perfect answer, but you can find meaningful patterns. For example, one of LarKC's initial projects is to take the location information of all the mobile phones in a city and use it to learn how the city infrastructure functions, hoping to find patterns and insights that may help regulate traffic, widen roads, build bridges, etc. Other projects involve drug, genetic, and cancer research with billions of "facts" drawn from huge databases. (Learn more at larkc.eu.)

Another approach is to take an old ontology that's been lying around for a few decades and bolt it onto Wikipedia. Begun in 1984, **Cyc** is a huge knowledge base that contains structured information about things and the relationships between them. It knows that Paris is the capital of France. It knows that a wheel is part of a larger structure. It knows that politicians can either be elected or appointed. It knows that an ambulance carries victims as well as emergency-response workers. With hundreds of thousands of terms and millions of assertions about those terms, Cyc is a ready-made knowledge model you can add to your own corporate ontology to make it smarter.

Need an ontology for your project? Check out **Swoogle,** a search engine that searches over 10,000 ontologies. The more ontologies that come online, the easier it will be to hook them up like Lego bricks to build a custom knowledge model for a given situation.

These mostly academic projects are online now and getting better all the time. For everyday commonsense reasoning, it's best if we all contribute to a single model than if we have disparate similar models that can't grow to the same scale (think WikiKnowledgePedia). A big, general ontology like this can hook to your company's ontology to better categorize and define and give structure to your knowledgebase.

One Ontology to Rule Them All?

People are building a surprising number of ontologies to help connect the world's data and build knowledge models in various domains: physics, biology, art, music, emergency services, banking, and so forth. But will there be an overarching ontology that links them all together? Can you imagine a "top ontology" that all ontologies can plug into, helping us contextualize the entire world of human knowledge?

The people at Umbel.org can, and they have built it. UMBEL (for Upper Mapping and Binding Exchange Layer) is a **subject backbone** for the semantic web. It's a set of longitude-latitude coordinates for topics, with 21,000 subjects, carefully distilled from hundreds of thousands of subjects in the Cyc ontology, and about 1.5 million "facts" about the world, also derived from Cyc. UMBEL could help build a smart search engine by connecting a number of knowledge models (ontologies) together. (Learn more at **Umbel.org** and **MKBergman.com**.)

What's Next

There are times when it's appropriate to have strict control over our metadata, there are times when a bunch of ad hoc tags are the best you can do, and there is great promise in the middle – in fuzzy ontologies that keep trying to model the world but never get it quite right. That's progress. On that continually shifting framework, we will build the semantic web, and it will continue to get better and better and better. Tim O'Reilly sums it up on his O'Reilly Radar blog:

> Don't ask users to provide structure unless it's useful to them. Design your applications in such a way that structure is generated without extra effort on the user's part. And mine structure that already exists, even if it's messy and inefficient.

Ontologies will make a huge difference to businesses and consumers, even if they don't know they are using them. They are already doing jobs in the auto industry that no other system can do. They are the only way to encode all our individual tastes, desires, and preferences. They will serve as a flexible way to interact with the products, services, media, and people in our lives.

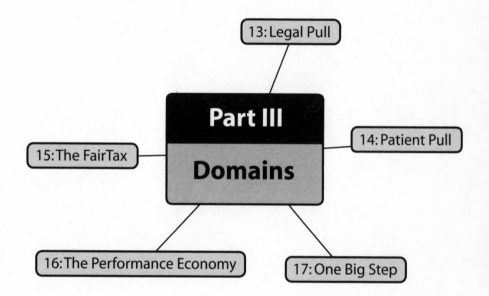

13: Legal Pull

Part III

Domains

14: Patient Pull

15: The FairTax

16: The Performance Economy

17: One Big Step

13: Legal Pull

Pull Concept: Semantic Building Blocks

> *The problem is no longer getting lawyers on the Net, but making them productive once they get there.*
>
> **– Jerry Lawson**

TODAY, IF YOU LOOKED AT A VENN DIAGRAM showing semantics (unambiguous terminology with precise meanings) and the world of legal writing, you would see two almost separate circles with a narrow sliver of overlap.* Ever so slowly, that overlap is starting to grow. Someone once told me that legislators *prefer* to write laws that different people can interpret in different ways, to give them wiggle room with their constituents. If laws were written clearly and unambiguously, they couldn't make everyone happy. By making bills 700 pages long and mixing gun control with credit card legislation, they are usually able to incorporate something for everyone.

As I wrote in my 1999 book *Futurize Your Enterprise*, someday we'll

---

* Lawyers are quick to disagree, saying they need special "terms of art" and complicated language to make documents more clear, rather than less. But there are many complications with interpretation of legal language, and even a single comma can have drastic consequences for one party or another.

separate the legal semantics (meaning) from the legal syntax (wording), and then we'll make the semantics machine-readable. That day has not arrived. In my research for this book, I got in touch with practically everyone in the world working on this problem, and only one project had any results to show. The rest are in research papers, proposals, and a few pilot projects that have just gotten started. While the need is great and billions of dollars are at stake, people working in legal semantics have very little funding and get almost no attention from the legal community. I include this chapter in the hope that it will help encourage people to get involved and make the next ten years more productive.

Semantics Versus Syntax

For too long, the legal world has encapsulated meaning by writing specific words, and the words are seen as the law, rather than simply the embodiment of the true intentions of the lawmakers in solving particular problems. My goal is to separate the legal intent, context, and meaning from the actual words written. Consider this example, from the office of the Consumer Credit Commissioner in Texas:

Before	After Simplification
Upon any such default, and at any time thereafter, Secured Party may declare the entire balance of the indebtedness secured hereby, plus any other sums owed hereunder, immediately due and payable without demand or notice, less any refund due, and Secured Party shall have all the remedies of the Uniform Commercial Code.	If I break any of my promises in this document, you can demand that I immediately pay all that I owe.

Both paragraphs mean the same thing, but they say it differently. The law in Texas recognizes these two statements as valid expressions of the same underlying concept (some legal systems don't). You can express the same concept in many different ways, using different words and languages. You could also express it in a way that a computer program can understand; that would be a **semantic representation** of the concept. If, rather than writing a contract, you could construct a contract using **semantic building blocks**, then you could render that contract in complex legalese, simplified English, simplified French, etc. This is how it's done today in business reporting using XBRL – and it should be how we write most contracts tomorrow.

Many early projects are focusing on **text analytics**, inferring meaning from legal texts already written. They follow a four-step process to derive the rules from the written text:

1. Extract the working terms.

2. Define the working terms semantically.

3. Build a taxonomy or other structure that specifies the relationships and constraints among the working terms.

4. Re-specify the rules using the taxonomy.

The result, ideally, is a set of semantic rules that can then serve as the machine-readable version of the law. Lawmakers can load these legal concepts into a dictionary and make them available online. Eventually, there will be dictionaries, taxonomies, and ontologies for many areas of law.

Semantic Regulation

The European Union has a tremendous incentive to bring laws into some kind of cooperative if not unified framework. Laws in Europe are a patchwork quilt of paragraphs written in dozens of languages, many of which do the same things, or almost the same things. Since regulations are easier to translate into a common format than laws are, that's where most of the action is. Committees are investigating how different countries regulate things like pesticide use, waste disposal, and highway safety, and ways they can better coordinate these regulations. As Europe unites, more and more legal edifices collide, creating the urgent need for concordances that simplify life for everyone.

European Patent Organization

The European Patent Organization grants patents under various conventions and treaties that have arisen since long before the European Union started. At the moment, there is no such thing as a European patent.* You can submit one application, and the EPO will grant patents from as many of the member patent offices as you ask for. The office helps adjudicate disputes, but it serves as little more than a go-between among nations with different sets of laws.

Some researchers have focused on local building codes, hoping to build a set of unambiguous taxonomies or ontologies that encapsulate the rules. If the software that designs buildings also uses these semantic structures, then, like the FDIC call report, it will prevent violations of the code.

One company working on this is Solibri, which has developed a methodology and software for designing buildings using Building Information Modeling (see Chapter 9). The BIM standard lets designers check their work against formal structural and compliance definitions. It should save a lot of time and money as virtual design and construction become mainstream.

---

*Not for lack of trying. The European Community Patent was put to a vote of member states in 2004, in the hope of creating a unified structure by 2010. It failed and has not been resurrected.

Contracts

At many law firms, common documents like divorce filings, leases, employee agreements, wills, and many others are based on templates. Several companies make software that automates the cut-and-paste process, asking questions and then building a written contract, which you can then print. The most sophisticated of these refers to internal definitions of the law and can do logic checking. A company called Exari has a system that lets you indicate whether you want a bias toward one party or the other, or prefer a "neutral" option. These enterprise "solutions" are nothing more than document workflow automation, as found in several other industries circa 1995. None is truly semantic, and none is part of the semantic web. There are no conceptual building blocks, no reference dictionaries, no taxonomies, and almost no standards.*

Someday, things will change. Contracts will make use of our online data lockers, and the laws will be written semantically. You'll work with a lawyer to put a legal document together using logical building blocks. And here's the important part – the resulting contract will be a **semantic agreement**, not a paper document. If people's addresses change, they will change automatically in the contract. If you move to a new state, for example, the contract will tell you if your agreement has changed materially. If the laws or regulations change, both parties will be contacted to keep the agreement current. In fact, as both parties reach their business milestones, the semantic updates from their activities will automatically keep the contract current (something most contracts require and yet is rarely done). Someday, we'll even make use of i-cards to manage the day-to-day progress and information flow, all feeding back to the contract at the center of the deal.

---

* At **LegalXML.com**, you can learn about a few standards that have been developed, but they are hardly in use and still only good for document construction, not for building true semantic logic modules.

Let's take a clear example. Publishers and promoters (including movie studios) often have complicated agreements with their artists – authors, musicians, actors, and talent of various kinds. There are advances, royalties, bonuses, conditional sweeteners, sales commissions, and so on. It can take months to negotiate a complicated contract, and a single work (album, movie, concert) can have dozens of such contracts with thousands of decision points.

Now imagine the back office, which has to disambiguate people with the same names, deal with pseudonyms, and make payments to everyone according to various schedules, often spelled out in hard-to-read text in the middle of a thirty-page contract! In January they send 1099 forms to as many people as they can think of, just to be safe. This is a manual process. They are lucky if they don't make too many mistakes in one day.

If the contracts were assembled semantically, however, then *the contracts themselves* would become the input to the software, which would pay each person according to what work has been performed, authorizing a transfer of funds from one account to another, even under the most complex of conditions. The contract could also keep the talent up to date on what's been executed and what milestone is coming up. Each participant would view the process on his or her own semantic dashboard. The software would be simpler than today's, and the results would be far more accurate. If anything important changed, everything would update automatically and the payments wouldn't skip a beat.

If you can imagine that kind of hardworking contract for talent, imagine something similar for your investments, school enrollment, driver's license, employment agreement, insurance, rent, day care, purchasing, travel, and other aspects of your life. Contracts are, both implicitly and explicitly, involved in much of what we do every day. Our tools should help us tag our way through these activities, help us keep our commitments, and prevent surprises.

Semantic Knowledge Models for Law

If you have symptoms, you can go to WebMD.com to get information about your condition and treatment for it. What if you have a legal problem? How can you find the information you need?

Today, the best you can do is keyword search, and this is a good example of where keyword search fails. If you're doing research on a patent application, you will find several patent databases you can search, but finding exactly what you're looking for, or learning that it doesn't exist, is almost impossible.

Where are the semantic building blocks? Where is all the linked data? Where are the cloud-based legal resources for all to share? We need in the legal field what John Wilbanks is doing at Science Commons – making everything semantically discoverable and hooking it to common vocabularies so we can find everything on a certain topic and query it. Then the **open legal web** will emerge, allowing people to find related cases, experts, statutes, rulings, and regulations. I would love to tell you that people are working on these things – building the foundations of semantic legal tools for the twenty-first century – but the silence is deafening. Professors with grant proposals and entrepreneurs with business plans can't get them funded. Fortunately, rather than ending this chapter on a down note, I have two real-world examples that will encourage any readers who might want to become part of the solution.

Digital Signatures

The signature of both parties makes a contract binding. Digital signatures are an important layer of the semantic web, and they are already here. A digital signature:

Seals the document, to assure that nothing is changed after signing,

Can't be forged or copied,

Can't be removed from the document,

Authenticates the person signing,

Is legally binding in North America and Europe,

Is safer than a handwritten signature,

Can include a digital watermark or handwritten signature image to remind others that the document has been signed and sealed, and

Saves at least $5 per signature over paper signatures.[27]

The most common use of this technology so far is in browsers for conducting secure transactions, like secure checkout for shopping. Digital signatures have been slow in coming but are now getting traction. We're starting to see them become part of the workflow infrastructure. Companies like EchoSign now have systems for document sign-off that shave days and weeks off the approval process. Companies like LinkedIn have now switched almost entirely to internal e-signatures.

In Europe, many countries require anyone filing a government document online to use a digital signature. Companies responding to requirements by the FDA and other agencies are now installing digital signature software and saving money. When the data never moves, it will make sense to sign a document and leave it signed and encrypted in the same place it was written – forever.

Copyright: The Story of Creative Commons

Launched in 2001 by Lawrence Lessig, Creative Commons is a nonprofit that lets people modify the terms of their copyright without having to wait for copyright laws to change. When you create anything, whether it's a song, an essay, a poem, a photograph, a video, or a program, you automatically have very restrictive rights – "all rights reserved" – in the United States and many other countries.* Today's laws don't allow the creator to give liberal licenses for noncommercial use without express written permission, so Lessig created a framework of licenses (agreements) that works on top of our existing legal structure.

Creative Commons allows people to specify that "some rights are reserved." This enables collaborative work, both commercial and noncommercial. You can attach the following conditions to your work:

> **Attribution.** Others can copy, distribute, display, or perform your work without asking or paying, but only if they give you credit.

> **Noncommercial.** Others can copy, distribute, display, or perform your work without asking or paying, but only for noncommercial purposes.

> **No derivative works.** Others can copy, distribute, display, or perform verbatim copies of your work without asking or paying, but they can't make any derivative works based on it.

> **Share alike.** Others can distribute derivative works under a license identical to the one you have chosen.

Various combinations of these conditions give you a **Creative Commons license** – a snippet of legal text you can attach to your work to specify the associated rights. These licenses let people make derivatives or collaborative works, or copy and use noncommercial works, without breaking the law. (Since January 24, 2009, the site WhiteHouse.gov uses Creative Commons licenses in all its content.)

---

* Different countries and regions have different laws. To keep up to date on what is being implemented where visit **monitor.creativecommons.org.**

Each Creative Commons license specifies the owner and the rights associated with that content using a controlled vocabulary in a standardized way. The license is embedded semantically in the work itself. Because Yahoo's search engine now understands these semantic standards, you can search all such photos anywhere on the web and filter for those with the specific rights you're looking for. When you copy and paste that image, the rights and attribution automatically come along as metadata. Even if you use images from twenty people and someone else then uses your work in her project, all the attributions will go along for the ride, creating a linked trail of rights that accumulate and apply to the new work. It's easy to trace back to the original creators of each part. This is true of songs, text, video, and other media – the license is embedded in the work itself and the new tools know how to use it.

Does this resonate with concepts from earlier chapters? Here we have a working format that encapsulates the legal framework right in the work itself. You generate the legal license as you copy and paste, mix and remix. Is this semantic? Yes. Is it on the web? Yes! Creative Commons licenses are leading components of the real semantic web.

Eventually, we will have a set of commercial licenses that do the exact same thing and pay royalties automatically, without any extra contract or collection work by either party. That's the pull paradigm at full force, metadata working for us in the background, so we can focus on more creative endeavors.

What's Next

As I mentioned in Chapter 8, your semantic will is going to be a living, executable document that can act on your behalf. As the environment changes, the document keeps up. The legalese that comes out of the printer will just be an artifact of the semantic building blocks that make the will so powerful. Someday, our adaptive legal documents will simply be an active information component of doing business – they will prevent us from doing anything illegal, especially when we don't know all the laws in our heads all the time. Someday, the legal linked data in the cloud will answer many of our legal questions. If the documents and data do all that for us, what will the lawyers do? They will do what they are trained to do – look for facts and help make decisions, rather than charge us for all the clerical work they do today.

14: Patient Pull

Pull Concept: Power Tagging

> *All that may come to my knowledge in the exercise of my profession or in daily commerce with men, which ought not to be spread abroad, I will keep secret and will never reveal.*
>
> – **Hippocratic Oath**

IN THE UNITED STATES, we do not just have the costliest health-care system in the world. We also have very little to show for it. The United States typically ranks near the bottom of developed countries for infant mortality, longevity, and health-care outcomes in general. Forty-seven million Americans are not insured. Countries that spend half as much on health care have better results. Canadians live an average of nearly three and a half years longer than we do, and the gap widens a little every year. Hospitals and doctors are incentivized to make more money, rather than take better care of patients. Medicare is now expected to start running a deficit by 2017.* As the baby boomers age and require more services, we'll have fewer people paying into the system. This is a bomb that is already exploding, and it's going to get worse before it gets better.

---

* See **pgpf.org** for details.

In this chapter, my plan is to add to whatever the government and insurance companies do in response to the health-care crisis. I'm going to paint the picture of how we can go from a doctor-push model to a patient-pull model. It will work with any health-care system in the world, empowering patients to take much more control over their health outcomes.

Doctor Push

Today, the doctor is the center of the health-care system. The doctor's time is precious; she needs to see as many patients as possible every day. There's no time to keep up with all the new medical research and developments, or patients' outcomes. The doctor looks at the chart, looks at the patient, writes something in the chart, sends the patient off with a treatment, then goes to the next patient. In general, doctors don't get paid more for helping people. They get paid for bringing revenues to the hospital.

The doctor reports to the insurance company. The insurance company rejects invoices for the slightest error – in billing, not in diagnosis or treatment. Doctors must continually resubmit to get paid. At the heart of this scheme is a book of **insurance codes** that gives a number to each procedure, each piece of equipment, and each of the hospital supplies used. Knowing that a certain plan won't reimburse a certain procedure, the doctor will simply substitute one that will, so she can get paid. More than a few doctors use the codes to get paid more than they would otherwise, often because they aren't reimbursed fairly in the first place. Gaming the system is convenient, quick, and common. One study, by the Centers for Medicare and Medicaid Services, found that over 48 percent of codes submitted had errors. Several studies have shown that when insurance companies reduce payment for certain codes, doctors compensate by finding new codes to bill, keeping overall payment levels about the same. Most patient records, whether on paper or in a computer, are at least partially wrong, and everyone knows it.*

Insurance companies don't care about wellness or recovery. Insurance companies try to maximize premiums and minimize payments. More than a third of the over $2 trillion we spend on health care goes to the administration of the system – moving real paperwork or its electronic counterpart. It seems the whole system would function much better if only there were no patients to gum it up.

The Rise of the E-Patient

Medicine has become too complex to be left to doctors. Hundreds of thousands of patients are unhappy with the time they spend with doctors and the information they receive from them. Doctors cannot be expected to keep up with the latest information on everything, even in their own fields. Online, in the real world, even in the halls of Congress, educated patients are starting to change the balance of power.

According to the Pew Foundation, 80 percent of Internet users have researched a medical issue online. In 2006, an estimated 93 million looked up health information online. People with rare or difficult conditions are the most determined searchers. Those most frustrated with the system often start their own web sites or nonprofits to fill an unmet need. Some of these sites become the single best authority on that condition anywhere. Sites like Endometriosis.org, PatientsLikeMe.com, and MichaelJFox.org are started by patients who want to help others deal with the medical system. Members share their research, their ex-

---

* In one of the most famous cases, Dave deBronkart imported his health records into Google Health, only to learn that all the codes had given him life-threatening conditions he didn't really have. He continues to blog about his experience surviving cancer at **e-Patients.net**, a site he cofounded.

perience, their doctor recommendations, and anything else that might support the cause. Some of these online communities have also become the best places for medical researchers to find human subjects with specific conditions. Doctors now routinely learn from them. There's the power shift: Just as we saw with products and books, patients (consumers) are quickly becoming *providers* of health-care information.

Today, the format for all this new information is mostly text. It's in blogs, Wikipedia articles, online magazine articles, comments, online communities, anecdotes, and so on. There are also dozens of online services where patients can store their health data, but they are all at a fairly primitive state and have very little momentum. How will all this prosumer activity improve health care in the age of the semantic web?

Health Blogging

I asked that question of my brother, Rob Siegel, a cardiologist in New York City. We were discussing the power shift from push to pull in medicine. I said, "Wouldn't it be great if you knew what happened to patients between appointments?"

"Absolutely," he said. "People come back six weeks later, and I have no idea whether they have actually taken their medication. Noncompliance is one of the biggest challenges doctors face. People forget to take their meds, then three days before the appointment they'll start taking them again, so they can say they have been. In reality, I have very little idea what goes on between appointments, and it matters."

"Let's suppose," I say, "that every patient now has an online data locker. All the patient's health history and records are there. The patient has plenty of privacy and security protection, so he can give you access only to what you need to treat him. Furthermore, he's actively involved in the process of learning about his health, recordkeeping, and understanding his options."

"A great idea, but only a few hospitals or insurance plans have managed to get patients enrolled in using them so far."

"After you write him a prescription," I continue, "he enters it into the health section of his personal data locker, which checks for any potential adverse drug reactions."

"It's a serious problem. In the United States, there are more than 2 million adverse drug reactions and 130,000 deaths per year from doctors prescribing drugs not knowing all the other drugs a patient is taking. We've tried many different approaches, including electronic patient records, yet we still haven't managed to reduce the number of deaths from misprescribing. In fact, the number keeps increasing. How is the data locker going to be the solution?"

"Suppose now that every day your patient keeps you up to date on how he's doing, so you can log in and see each day what's going on with him since you wrote that prescription."

"Let's see," he says, looking skeptical, "I have something like a thousand patients I'm trying to help, and now they are all health blogging? I have to go read all their health entries? Do I need to follow them on Twitter, too?"

"Oh no," I say, smiling. "They're not health blogging. They're power tagging."

"Power tagging?"

Power Tagging

In the future, today's e-patient will be tomorrow's semantically powered patient. Doctors will use a new semantic protocol that actually spells out treatments rather than just giving a code for each step. It will be similar to the US GAAP taxonomy, describing common treatments and their potential variations. It will hook directly to the patient in two ways: via sensors and devices and via questionnaires giving semantic feedback.* Here's how it will work in a typical scenario: The doctor prescribes a drug or combination of drugs. At the pharmacy the patient picks up a prepackaged "smart pillbox." The pharmacy has already checked the interactions of all the drugs in each box. The box has a compartment for each dose of pills, and it knows when it's been opened. It has a display and can ask patients to answer questions before they can open the container, like rating their pain or symptom level on a scale from 1 to 5. The system also sends the patient an email asking specific questions with checkbox-style answers that come from a controlled vocabulary. Answers go to the doctor and into the patient's data locker. The system and doctor can adjust dosage or bring the patient in if necessary. By communicating with patients *during* treatment, doctors can prevent weeks of misery and relapse, and they can catch new problems early.

Several of these semantic monitoring tools already exist. The smart pillbox has been around since 1995 (see "The Pull Pillbox"). The online glucose monitor already sends several readings each day and asks the diabetes patient how much insulin she's injected herself with and how she is feeling. Digital thermometers and scales will feed their data to your electronic health record. There are blankets that can record and transmit heartbeat data. Patients can swallow a wireless sensor that reports on conditions as it travels through their bodies. Consumers will also have access to many more diagnostic tests at home. The results of all these tools will go straight into patients' data lockers, which will then feed into the physician's datastream about the patient.

Power tagging is recording real-time facts and events from the real world, using common formats and vocabularies in a format that means the same thing to all systems. We've already encountered it in several

---

* There are some common vocabularies, but almost no standards exist for common treatment protocols that would allow the power tagging I describe here – insurance companies see no need for them.

previous chapters. Power tagging is contextual – you do it on the spot, either regularly or as soon as something happens. Whether it's building your patient record, contributing to a project record, making a shopping list, or building an intranet, power tagging helps you keep your semantic web of information up to date and working for all the people around you. If everyone does it, the systems know what's happening in the real world and people can pull information through.

Health Connect

At Kaiser Permanente, more than 25 percent of members now use their personal health record, Health Connect. The site allows patients to view parts of their medical records, send clinical information to online tools, schedule appointments, request prescription refills, email their doctors, ask questions of pharmacists, and access tailored programs for behavior changes such as smoking cessation and weight management. The result of Kaiser's efforts is that office visits are down 26 percent and patients are more satisfied.

– **Arun Mohan and Gordon Moore**[28]

We will use a variety of automated tools, sensors, other people, and special-purpose devices that let us power-tag our way through our days. At appropriate times, our phones will display quick questions that take just a few seconds to answer. The answers will add up. Power tagging will lead to better outcomes. There will be many fewer adverse drug interactions. Doses will adjust automatically to prevent side effects. The system will recognize changes that indicate a yellow-flag condition ("monitor more closely") or a red-flag alert ("see patient immediately"). The system can automatically help the patient schedule a visit if things change unexpectedly.

Doctors will not only see all their patients' progress at a glance, but they will use this data to help find subpopulations that respond to the same medicine differently. By looking across an entire nation of patient data, doctors will see patterns in the data that guide research, help develop new drugs, and change policy. The more data we collect in standard formats, the better we can help researchers find the next treatment.

The Pull Pillbox

Dr. John Urquhart is trying to solve a problem: when people are on long-term medication, only 50 percent of patients still take their meds after the first year. Only 5 percent never miss a dose that first year. His company, Aardex Group, makes a smart pill container that knows and transmits every time it is opened. Developed originally for clinical trials, the MicroElectrical Mechanical Systems (MEMS) box has an LCD readout on the cover, so patients know their status as well. The data tell doctors how often the patient takes his or her meds and so can determine how much of the medication is actually in the bloodstream.

Over 400,000 patients have used the MEMS boxes, mostly for clinical trials. But within a few years, the boxes will report directly to a patient's own online health record. Doctors will see the patient's compliance history and the results on a daily basis. They can then adjust the dose of medication based on the feedback given, without a visit to the office. This is called measurement-guided medication management. It will become an important tool in helping patients pull their own medications through as they need them, and it will let doctors learn much faster which populations respond to treatments differently.

"There's a difference between nonperformance and nonadherence," Dr. Urquhart says. "Unfortunately, many doctors think all those numbers are boring! They say: 'I don't want to be involved in the micromanagement of my patient.'" There's also the risk of losing the "customer" to another doctor who won't nag them so much. The MEMS boxes, which were introduced in 1995, will become power tools when a new generation of data-aware doctors can prescribe them properly to a new generation of patients.

Once patients are power tagging, they will form their own research communities, reach out to drug and device companies, and pull new products through according to their needs. Patients will create online ecosystems of patient data that researchers can filter for trends, patterns, and new insights. The online data lockers will protect patients' identity and privacy, helping researchers identify and work with test subjects.

Power tagging for patients will start slowly, in places with progressive doctors and a strong information infrastructure. Early-adopter patients will help make the systems better. But in ten or fifteen years, I predict, the quality of health care will accelerate as a result of power tagging. Power tagging and personal data lockers are the platform for what comes next.

Individualized Medicine

"Predisease is the new disease," says Dr. Steven Murphy, who specializes in individualized medicine. "Most people come to the doctor's office when they have symptoms. We'll soon predict the possibility of, or actually detect, and in some cases even prevent many diseases years before a patient has any symptoms."

The age of individualized medicine, where drugs can be tailor-made to an individual's genome and biochemistry, has already started. Rather than using small-molecule drugs that enter many different cells, dosing each cell they encounter whether it needs it or not, new "big-molecule" therapies will go right where they are needed and complete their mission. This targeted approach uses molecular diagnostics to determine exactly which molecule, or combination of molecules, will do the job precisely, with few or no side effects.

This new science is called "proteomics." It's the study of proteins. Genes code for proteins. Specific genes make specific proteins, and certain gene combinations make other proteins. Proteins can have defects, become misfolded, combine with other proteins, convert one kind of protein into another, and so on. Almost all diseases are either a result of a gene that causes a protein to do the wrong thing or a defect in a protein that then self-replicates. Many autoimmune diseases are simply genes telling the body's cells to do their natural thing in overdrive, causing too much of an otherwise good thing. Genes and proteins give the signals for abnormal behavior. The more information we have about the genes and proteins in our bodies, the more we can build targeted protein-based drugs that neutralize problem cells with fewer side effects than the medicines we use now.

One arm of genetic medicine is to look at the genetics of the disease itself. For example, the HIV virus enters T cells at one of two different sites I'll call A and B. Today, patients with the version of HIV that enters at A take a drug called Maraviroc, which binds with that site on all the patient's T cells, effectively halting progression of AIDS. The FDA requires a positive test for that version of the virus before you can get a prescription for Maraviroc. A similar drug aimed at the version of the AIDS virus that enters at site B should be available within a few years.*

Most cancers have a genetic factor – certain people are more susceptible than others. The most common cancer among children and adolescents is Acute Lymphoblastic Leukemia (ALL). Thirty years ago, the prognosis for survival with chemotherapy was less than 10 percent. Today, genetic testing allows doctors to make a cocktail of drugs tailored to the type of ALL a child has, with many fewer side effects. As a result, the cure rate is now over 80 percent.

Chronic Myelogenous Leukemia (CML) is the result of a chromosomal error that fuses two proteins, producing an abnormal protein that causes a rapid increase in the number of white blood cells. A new drug called Gleevec binds to the abnormal protein and inhibits its action. For most patients, Gleevec has no side effects, a 95 percent survival rate for the first five years, and must be taken indefinitely to provide protection. In contrast with chemotherapy, it has been called a miracle drug.

---

* Maraviroc, like most other big-molecule drugs, may have side effects, but it's too early to tell. The question is not: "Does it have zero side effects?" The question is: "Are the results better and the side effects less problematic than the drugs we are using today?" So far, the benefits seem to outweigh the risks, and the FDA seems willing to approve drugs that show results with patients in clinical trials.

Many adverse drug reactions have a genetic basis. The FDA has already approved the AmpliChip cytochrome P450 test, which helps doctors decide which drugs and at what doses to give patients. Depending on a patient's genetic makeup, the liver metabolizes about half of all small-molecule drugs slowly, normally, or quickly. The molecular approach requires much less trial and error to get the right dose and has fewer side effects than the old approach. The FDA now recommends this test for many patients receiving certain drugs. When personalized therapies result in fewer side effects, patients more willingly comply with doctors' orders.

Researchers I spoke with said that in the next thirty years, big-molecule therapies will delay or cure many inherited diseases such as Alzheimer's, Huntington's chorea, and perhaps thousands of very rare genetic diseases. Diseases often have many subtypes; combination therapies will be common. Most cancer researchers are confident that the days of chemotherapy, radiation therapy, and surgery as the usual response are numbered.

In general, protein drugs are not magic bullets – they can and do have side effects. They will, however, be an important part of the physician's tool kit. For certain diseases they will eventually replace the small-molecule therapies we use today. Whether they will become mainstream outside of cancer and autoimmune diseases remains to be seen.

Our personal data lockers will store our sex, weight, body-mass index, blood type, ethnicity, family history, blood tests, and other data that already help our doctors modify prescriptions and doses. Within ten years, many people will have their entire genetic code and the genetic code of any disease agents living in their bodies. This will signal a new era in medicine, one the FDA is already gearing up for.

In the next twenty years, routine blood screens like those for certain ovarian and breast cancers already in use today will detect the molecular markers of disease long before patients develop symptoms. We'll know whether you are a candidate for a given preventive drug and how you will respond to a treatment even before you get it. New genetic tests help researchers screen populations for testing, speeding up the approval process. Researchers are starting to revisit older drugs that failed clinical trials because many of the people they tested randomly didn't have the correct genetic makeup.

Within five years, most newborns will get these genetic tests:

Cytochrome P450 (determines how quickly you metabolize two large classes of drugs)

Predisposition to certain cancers

Mitochondrial mutations

Full genome (as price comes down)

With power comes responsibility. We will need to manage our health information to a greater extent than we have, and we will be better off for it. Wouldn't you rather store your entire genome in your data locker, under your control, with your other health data, and give out as much as you want, when you want, to whom you want?

Patient Privacy

"When a patient walks in the door of a hospital, the hospital sees not just one dollar sign, but two," says Tim Sparapani, senior legislative counsel for the American Civil Liberties Union. "The first dollar is what they earn from treating the patient. The second is the amount they earn selling the information about the patient."[29]

The problem isn't that the laws don't protect patient privacy. In fact, state and federal laws specifically prohibit your health-care service providers from selling your data. The problem is that the industry and its lobbies, including the AMA, make so much money selling your data to drug companies that they simply ignore the laws. The Health Insurance Portability and Accountability Act (HIPAA), as amended by the Bush administration in 2003, was an industry lobbyist's dream, enabling data mining on a vast scale. It's still against the law, but every time you get a prescription filled at a pharmacy, that information is sold multiple times to many different buyers. More than 4 million pharmacies, corporations, insurers, government agencies, hospitals, self-insured employers, doctors, and others have access to your personal health information without giving you notice, even if you object. Practically the only person who doesn't have the right to take your data from the system is you.[30]

In the 1990s, Richard Dick founded Nex2, a company that built one of the largest drug-history databases in the world, with over 200 million Americans' five-year prescription histories updated every twenty-four hours by almost all pharmacies in the United States. This information helped insurance companies adjust their premiums to make sure they made money. The AMA was one of his closest allies. Dick paid the AMA to re-identify any prescriptions that didn't have doctors' names on them from its database of over 830,000 doctors (though pharmacies are usually very good at selling quality, complete data). In 2008, the AMA sold $47.6 million in "database products," which they don't break down further in their annual report, but much of it is physician data sold to drug companies without the consent of doctors or patients. Pharmacies do the same.

Drug companies buy the data so their reps have an accurate prescribing profile for every doctor they visit. Most reps are paid based on how much of their company's products their doctors prescribe. Drug companies pay about $.30 per prescription record. For $400 each, they can buy the ten-year history of more than 100 million Americans. Until 2006, doctors could not prevent drug sales reps from acquiring their

Patient Privacy Rights

After the Bush administration and the health industry lobby amended the original HIPAA privacy rule in 2003 to allow practically unlimited data mining of electronic patient records, Dr. Deborah Peel founded Patient Privacy Rights in 2004. Her mission: to educate Congress about the need to restore and strengthen Americans' longstanding health privacy rights, enforce the laws we have, and build an electronic health-care information technology infrastructure patients will be willing to use, knowing they can keep their health records private and control who can see and use them. Most Americans don't know their personal medical data is sold almost daily to any company that wants to pay.

Dr. Peel's web site and tireless advocacy command attention on Capitol Hill. Among her goals:

A nation of educated consumers who can advocate successfully for their right to health privacy

A strong national policy recognizing our right to health privacy, with safeguards to ensure and protect that right in federal statute

A successful, progressive health information technology industry that ensures that consumer control of personal health information is the cornerstone of product design

A "patient's bill of privacy rights," specifying the criteria that all systems must comply with to become certified

Learn more at **PatientPrivacyRights.org.**

prescription data. For this accomplishment, Dr. Clayton Christensen of Harvard Business School named Dick ". . . one of our most disruptive innovators." Prescription data mining alone is worth at least $2 billion annually in the United States,[31] with many well-known companies and health plans participating, and it's all illegal. Richard Dick sold his company to United Healthcare in 2002.

The answer to this shell game of metadata profiteering is **consent management**. While there are very few companies in this emerging service market, a notable start-up is You Take Control. This company enables patients to disclose their information to health-care providers on an as-needed basis. The company was founded by none other than Richard Dick, who now regrets his former role in health-care data mining. (Learn more at **y-t-c.com.**)

Every step is a battle against huge vested interests. The Genetic Information Nondiscrimination Act of 2008 was *supposed* to prevent health insurers from ever seeing your genetic data, but the drug lobby and the Bush administration insisted that employers and insurers have a right to see this data, even if they can't use it to fire you (though they *can* use it to deny life insurance). Companies that do genetic testing are allowed to sell their data to third parties with no consent management and little oversight.

In 2009, President Obama signed the American Recovery and Reinvestment Act, which prohibits the sale of patients' medical records without express written consent to the sale, requires an audit trail of who sees what information, sets standards for encryption, and more. This law will make it much harder for health-care providers, insurers, health IT vendors, pharmacy benefits managers, and pharmacies to sell our personal information and for aggregators to acquire and profit from the sale of our records. But the fight isn't over until each state's attorney general decides to start enforcing the law and manages to scare the pharma giants into finding another way to measure success. For now, the battle is state by state. The Davids have won a few battles, but they have a long way to go before winning the war against the Goliath drug and data mining industries.

It won't be long before genetic sequencing is affordable. Patients should be aware: insurers and employers should *never* have access to your genetic data. They will only use it to benefit themselves. Consent management and a patients' bill of privacy rights will become the foundation on which millions of Americans manage their own health information from their personal data lockers.

What's Next

To fix health care, we have to stop treating the symptoms. We must fix the systemic issues: how to pay for it, incentivize people properly, reward prevention, discourage waste, and handle information. Whatever we do in health care, we must realize that just making our paper documents electronic will make things worse. We need laws that enable the proper sharing of data. It seems that legislators, health-care providers, and patients all address medical informatics only when they *need* to, further extending a broken system, rather than planning for and implementing a coherent strategy.

It's going to be tricky. There is very little alignment of interest. One party usually loses. Like the casinos in Las Vegas, the industry has most of the information and is in the business of winning. That will have to change. In the pull era, every undergraduate should take a course in **personal data management** that includes a section on gathering, keeping, and using personal health records.

15: The FairTax

Pull Concept: Putting the Rules into the Transactions

> *Putting people into homes, though a desirable goal, shouldn't be our country's primary objective. Keeping them in their homes should be the ambition.*
>
> **— Warren Buffett**

IN CHAPTER 5, I SHOWED how governments can put the rules right into the transactions themselves, rather than try to dictate human behavior. Here, I want to show a very real example of that concept, and at the same time chop about $1 trillion of waste out of the U.S. economy. It's based on the proposed Fair Tax Act of 2009 (HR 25, S 296), which would eliminate the IRS, the income tax, and the accounting profession. This isn't a chapter on tax reform. My goal is to show the wastefulness of pushing, the benefits of pulling, and how the principles of pulling can play an important role in our economic recovery. (You'll find references for all the claims in this chapter on the fair tax section of **ThePowerofPull.com**.)

The U.S. economy generates about $13 trillion annually. The government's budget every year is about $3 trillion. Besides excise, import, and other taxes, the government collects about $2.2 trillion in income taxes. To do this, the IRS directly employs about 100,000 people and spends

$10 billion annually. The tax code is a 60,000-page document that contains enough loopholes to keep tens of thousands of accountants busy. Filing tax documents and consulting on tax strategy amounts to more than $400 billion of economic activity annually.

The general rule in taxation is: You get less of what you tax more; you get more of what you tax less. In the United States, we tax income. You could say we push people to (reluctantly) report what they make and to pay a percentage in tax. One result is that people don't save. Another is that people avoid paying taxes whenever possible. Estimates of the underground, non-tax-paying economy in the United States are $1.5 to $3 trillion. Collection isn't easy. The IRS estimates that in 2001 it collected $365 billion less than it was owed. American businesses and wealthy individuals keep around $10 trillion in assets offshore specifically to avoid paying taxes on it.

Everyone has his own personal favorite example of how convoluted our tax code has become. Because I collect royalties from a software firm in Germany, every two years I must verify that I'm a resident of the United States, as follows:

> The Internal Revenue Service (IRS) procedure for requesting a certificate of residency (Form 6166) from the Philadelphia Accounts Management Center is the submission of Form 8802, Application for United States Residency Certification. Use of the Form 8802 is mandatory. A user fee will be charged to process all Forms 8802 received with a postmark date on or after November 1, 2006.*

About 250 million entities file income tax returns each year. Do people get their taxes right? No. The vast majority of U.S. households overpay and get a refund check of $2,429 on average.

---

* There are twelve pages of instructions for Form 8802. The fee is $35. Estimated average time for filling out and submitting Form 8802 is *over five hours*.

American workers pay at least 15 percent in income tax, plus 7.65 percent in payroll taxes, which are matched by corporations. This amount is already built into the price of every product or service any company provides. Corporations do not pay income taxes; they simply pass on their tax burden by building it into the price of their goods and services. Ultimately, consumers pay all these taxes – with after-tax dollars!

All but one of the thirty countries in the Organization for Economic Co-operation and Development (OECD) have adopted some kind of VAT – a value-added or general sales tax. The only country that hasn't is the United States. Furthermore, many estimate that the coming retirement boom will bankrupt the U.S. government in our lifetime.* We all need to find an engine of economic growth to earn our way out of the collective debt we have to our retiring baby boomers.

The FairTax

Almost any tax system would be more efficient than the one we have. If you compare alternative approaches, you'll come across the FairTax, a consumption-based tax that, I believe, is a better approach than a value added tax (VAT) to raising the money the federal government needs. In fact, the FairTax is the pull approach to raising revenue for the federal government. The FairTax eliminates:

The IRS

The income tax and payroll tax

Self-employment taxes

---

* I encourage all readers to visit **IOUSAthemovie.com** and **PGPF.org**.

Capital gains tax

Gift and estate taxes

Luxury tax

The alternative minimum tax

Corporate taxes

Almost 100 percent of the tax accounting industry

Tax "benefits" under the current tax law

Under the FairTax, the government would:

Impose a 23 percent inclusive (30 percent exclusive) national sales tax on all new goods and consumer services.*

Pay retailers, service providers, and state governments a fee of 0.25 percent each for collecting tax revenues and remitting them to the federal government; as a result, they will *want* to collect these taxes.

Raise slightly more than the current system in an average year.

Send a bimonthly "prebate" check to every registered American, amounting to about $2,300 per year.

I'm not going into the details – the actual bill is 132 pages long. The basic idea is to add an amount of federal tax to local sales taxes already being collected (in most states), and the right number turns out to

---

* If you bought something for $1, you would pay an added $.30 for a total of $1.30. Using the 23 percent inclusive figure makes it comparable to the income tax percentage figures, and 30 percent makes it comparable to sales tax. You can call it a 30 percent tax if you like. It still raises the same amount of money as the income tax does.

be 23 percent to collect the same amount as the government collects today.*

A few things to note:

> Some people think the FairTax is regressive. It is not. It's more progressive than our current income tax. Those spending the most pay the most.

> Spending is more consistent from year to year than earnings.

> Prices paid at the register would not change that much, as corporations would soon reduce their prices by the amount they currently pass through (which is more than 23 percent). Prices could actually go down in many cases.

> The FairTax would raise the same amount of money as our current tax system does, but without the $400 billion in tax planning and preparation costs.

> Retailers and service providers *make money* under the FairTax; they have no incentive to cheat and incur fines. Evasion would be far less than it is under the current system.

> Only new home sales are taxed. Most people, especially first-time homebuyers, buy a used home and would therefore pay no tax on the purchase or on any interest paid on loans.

Here are just a few of the benefits:

---

* Recall from Chapter 8 that the best way to apply this tax is to impose a tax of *x*, where *x* has its own special place online and is initially set to 23. If the government wants to raise more or less money, it could just change that one number and all the cash registers in the country would respond immediately.

No more accountants.

Americans take home 100 percent of their paychecks.

With the prebate, the tax is quite progressive. Rich people who spend will pay much more than those who save and don't buy as much. A couple with two $35,000 jobs currently pays 21.3 percent of their income to the federal government; under the FairTax, they would pay 11.6 percent.

Tourists to the United States pay a significant part of the federal revenues (as we normally do when purchasing goods or staying in hotels in their countries, less the VAT).

All families immediately save all the money they currently spend planning for and preparing income tax.

The United States would become a job magnet, as it would be a tax haven for corporations, which won't have to pay payroll taxes.

Offshore assets of $10 trillion would repatriate, resulting in increased spending.

Illegal workers would pay the same 23 percent sales tax but would *not* receive the prebate checks.

In this way, the government would *pull* revenues out of consumers in a way that puts consumers much more in control. Consumers would no longer have that helpless feeling as their work rewards are sucked away, but instead would have the power to decide whether to purchase or save. That shift would result in a much more entrepreneurial economy, because most businesses are small businesses, and today's tax system hits small businesses hardest with the administration and disincentive of paying withheld income taxes.

The Simplification Movement

We can see one clear trend in this book: We are doing things so backwardly that it's often better to blow something up completely than to try to make it better. The IRS is a great place to start. The FairTax already has considerable momentum. It has over fifty congressional cosponsors. It has many grassroots groups helping to educate legislators and voters across the country. Many people misunderstand it, because it takes some time to understand the details. As a progressive liberal, I am a strong supporter of the plan. I hope both Democrats and Republicans will take the time to learn more about it and tell their friends about it. Once the United States adopts a smart taxation mechanism like this, other countries will follow, and that could lead to an era of smart and simple tax policy.

The FairTax is much simpler than a VAT. It fits right in to the semantic web and the pull paradigm. As we saw with the FDIC call report, putting the rules into the transactions can save enough money to pay for the new system the first time you do it. I believe switching to the FairTax would pay dividends quickly and play an important role in making our government more efficient. In 2009, we finally phased out analog TV signals over the airwaves. This single bill will phase out the IRS and most accountants in a single year as well.

I hope I've raised more questions than I've answered. Your next stop is **FairTax.org** to learn more.

16: The Performance Economy

Pull Concept: Alignment of Company and Customer Interest

> *The problem isn't just silos and walled gardens. The problem is the defaulted belief system that gives us silos and walled gardens in the first place. In that system, suppliers believe that the best customers and users are captive ones.*
>
> **– Doc Searls**

I REMEMBER SEEING AN AD for Merrill Lynch some years ago, and the voice-over said something to the effect that it was different from other investment firms. The actress playing an investor said, "I can choose whether I want to pay commissions the old-fashioned way, or switch to an *asset-based management fee*," which was supposed to show how progressive the company was. I wondered whether the executives behind this piece of prime-time legerdemain were ashamed of themselves. I was certainly ashamed for them. They only cared about their commissions; they didn't care if the customer made money or not. They still don't.

At some point, the power shift is going to become infectious, and this is going to go far beyond data and software and web sites. It's going to change the deal we strike with our customers, and that will change the entire economy. Think about it – a few graduate students built the first web browser. They defined a common format for documents that was simple and easy to program. And that turned into the World Wide Web, which changed business and our economy profoundly. It empowered customers in ways we never could have predicted in the early 1990s. Now we're about to go through an even more disruptive transformation, one where customers can see all offers and deep industry intelligence as easily as the most seasoned industry insider.

Pull leads to performance. Just as pulling metadata aligns your customer's information with yours, **in the performance economy, your company's economics are aligned with your customer's**. While the push economy is based on processes, the performance economy is based on outcomes. It's not your grandmother's metadata, and it isn't your father's business model.

Still Doing Things the Hard Way

Not all industries put the customer at the center. Many are still resting on the old push mechanics. In the United States:

Average outstanding credit card debt for households that do not pay their balance in full every month was over $17,000 at the end of 2008.[32]

Americans pay over $4 billion in ATM surcharges (the average surcharge is $1.78 per transaction, while the cost to the bank is $0.27).[33]

In 2004, Americans wrote over 40 billion paper checks,[34] resulting in $38 billion in service charge fees, half of that for overdrawn accounts.[35]

Paperwork costs for our health-care system now exceed $400 billion – more than $1,000 per citizen.[36]

In the performance economy, companies that focus on results for their customers set the pace. Their systems are tied into their customers' systems, so they can work together in real time. They pay their suppliers in real time as goods arrive, rather than holding back payment as long as possible. Groups of employees can easily work with customers, partners, even competitors, without much overhead.

In the performance economy, your job is to solve your customers' problems. You're not selling doors and windows; you're helping build a hospital or an office building or a home. Each of these problems has its own set of challenges, all of which are now online in a common semantic workspace. You may help them use *fewer* doors or windows, or whatever your product is, because that could make for a better, safer hospital. And that's better for everyone.

In the performance economy, the outcome matters and determines your reward. That's hardly the case on Wall Street or with your cable company. When was the last time your consultant said she'd like to be paid a percentage of the amount you make (or save) with her advice? What if *you* were paid according to the outcomes you achieve?

The Performance Business Model

In 2007, Britain's national health system warned it would no longer pay for Johnson & Johnson's expensive cancer drug Velcade. To keep the drugs flowing, J&J now offers a money-back guarantee: if Velcade fails to shrink a patient's tumors after a trial treatment, the company promises to pay the health system for the cost of that patient's drug.

In the United States, people with osteoporosis (chronic bone loss) suffer an estimated 1.5 million fractures annually. Bone fractures are the gold standard for measuring the effectiveness of any drug that claims to slow, stop, or reduce osteoporosis. In 2009, Procter and Gamble made a deal with insurer Health Alliance: Health Alliance would supply Actonel, a monthly pill that costs $100 each, to its patients who received prescriptions for osteoporosis medication. In return, if any of these patients subsequently had a bone fracture, P&G would reimburse Health Alliance up to $30,000 for a hip fracture and $6,000 for a wrist fracture.

Merck struck a deal with insurer Cigna to benefit patients with type 2 diabetes. The drug company will offer bigger discounts if Cigna can incentivize patients to take two Merck drugs, Januvia and

Janumet, regularly. This in turn should incentivize the insurer to capture the information from patients (power tagging) so they can verify that the pills were taken at the right times and in the proper doses. Astonishingly, Merck has offered additional discounts to Cigna if the insurer can prove that patients' blood sugar is better controlled, regardless of how that result is achieved. As we move toward evidence-based and outcome-based medicine, we will need more measurable and accurate information from patients, all enabled by people's online data lockers.

These last two deals, announced just as I am putting the finishing touches on the manuscript for this book, point the way toward the per-formance economy. Drug companies are looking for more performance deals with insurers so they can keep their drugs prescribed. A cynical view might suggest that the drug companies have merely made an ac-tuarial calculation and view the payments and discounts as part of the cost of marketing an expensive drug. With margins like that, the com-pany can afford to build in the cost of a few fractures.* But a more op-timistic view would say that at least some of these deals are being made because a company actually stands behind the outcome of its product. It's far too early to spot a trend here, but it's an encouraging sign. Can you imagine a pay-for-performance deal with your customers?

---

* Just for fun, let's do the math, assuming Actonel works no better than a sugar pill. Ac-cording to WHO FRAX, the fracture risk-assessment tool, the ten-year hip fracture risk of an American Caucasian woman age 55 with three out of six risk factors and no loss of bone density is less than 1 percent. If 100 of these women take Actonel monthly for ten years, the company takes in 100 x 100 x 120 = $1.2 million; if one has a fracture, the cost to the company is $30,000. The risk of an American woman age 65 with a reasonable amount of bone loss already (bone mineral density T-score of -2.0) and three risk factors is 5.7 percent, so over the next ten years, the company would take in another $1.2 million and pay out $170,000. For the third decade, women at age 75 with a bit more bone loss (BMD T-score of -3) have a fracture risk of 47 percent, for a payout of $1.4 million – a loser. If P&G can get women to start taking the pill by age 60, the offer is a win for the company whether it reduces the patient's risk of fracture or not.

Listings and Bias

Looking for a dentist? In America, 1-800-Dentist offers highly detailed (semantic) information about dentists and lets consumers compare dentists head to head. Consumers can "drill down" to learn more about a dentist's background, practice, or capabilities. Dentists listed have a current license, are board-certified in their specialties, and they must have malpractice insurance and other appropriate insurances. And it's all free to the consumer.

Who pays for the service? Dentists, of course. If you don't pay, you aren't listed. According to CNN, participating dentists pay from $6,000 to $18,000 per year for these consolidated marketing services, and if customers complain, the company "investigates" the complaints.

Contrast this with Angie's List, a community of over 750,000 consumers who *pay* to learn about service providers in many categories. Not only can service providers not enter themselves in the database, but only a paying member can suggest a company for the list. The list initially focused on home improvement and home care, but it now has extensive lists of doctors, medical facilities, and other service providers.

Which of these referral services is part of the performance economy? Will people really pay for unbiased listings? Since listings are metadata and since the semantic web will let us find what we are really looking for on the open web, it's likely that both these business models will eventually fade. What will likely prevail?

A listing is a kind of offer. In the world of passive commerce, not only can we find the offers easily, but our data lockers will negotiate with them and filter them automatically, bringing us only those offers that have the best chance of giving us what we really want. In this world, the companies that produce "leads" will need to find a different way to make money than they do today. They'll have to add unbiased value to a transaction or go away.

The Performance Social Network?

LinkedIn is a social network with over 38 million members and hundreds of employees. Most members pay nothing, but you can get added services by signing up for a business account and paying a monthly fee. It takes three button clicks to sign up for the subscription-based business service. Three clicks. However, once you are a business member, you may want to downgrade back to a free membership. How easy is that? I'll let the LinkedIn customer-service rep answer that question:

> To downgrade to a lower premium subscription level or to cancel your premium account and switch to a free personal account, follow the steps below:
>
> Click on "Account & Settings" found in the upper right-hand side of the home page.
>
> Click on "Compare Account Types" and identify the account type that best fits your needs.
>
> Click on "Customer Service" link found at the bottom of the page.
>
> Click on "Ask Customer Service" tab on the "Customer Service Center" page.
>
> Enter your account's primary email address in "Contact Information."
>
> Select "Premium Accounts" from the "Category" dropdown under "My question is about."
>
> In the "Subject" type "Downgrade My Subscription" (if you want a lower level premium subscription) or "Cancel My Subscription" (if you want to just keep the free personal account).
>
> In the "Question" text box, identify what type of account you want to end up *with* through this request. For example,

"I would like to change to Business Plus account" or "I only want a free personal account."
Click on "Continue."

This from a company that has adopted digital signatures on *all* internal documents. I'm pretty sure they can add a "Downgrade my account" button and have it working within a few days, but the company responded to my question by saying, "This is a feature that we hope to have added to the site in the future."

Furthermore – and this is a lesson for most online services – if you sign up for a business account with a monthly charge, your monthly charge will take place without a courtesy email letting you know you're paying for the service. It turns out that many people who sign up for recurring charges aren't aware that the charges are recurring, and there have been several class-action lawsuits as a result.

Facebook has stumbled several times in going against customer wishes. Each time, the members have used the company's tools against it to gang up and make the changes they want.

Acquiring new customers is usually much more expensive than retaining old ones. It pays to make sure your customer loves doing business with you.

The Net Promoter Score

In the performance economy, the brand doesn't own the customer – the customers own the brand. In his book *The Ultimate Question*, Fred Reichheld asks the key question: Would you recommend this company's products or services to a friend? As Reichheld explains on his web site, **theultimatequestion.com**:

Most companies assume they're giving customers what they want. Usually, they're kidding themselves. Bain & Company recently surveyed 362 firms and found that 80 percent believe they deliver a "superior experience" to customers. But when Bain asked their customers, they said only 8 percent are really delivering.

Bain dubbed the 80 percent the "believers" and the 8 percent the "achievers." Whatever the nomenclature, this ten-to-one ratio suggests a startling gap between those who think they're doing right by the customer and those who truly are.

Reichheld's measurement tool is the Net Promoter Score (NPS), which subtracts negative "detractors" from positive "promoters" of the brand, as a percentage of total customers, to come up with a net percentage of customers who actively promote the brand. (For example, if 8 percent are fanatic promoters but 3 percent are actively saying bad things about the company, the NPS is 5.) Most companies are lucky to have an NPS in the low positive single digits. (I suspect many well-known brands' scores are negative numbers.)

As I write this, Satmetrix has just released a report of several online brands and their Net Promoter Scores:[37]

Company	NPS
Apple	77
Amazon	74
Costco	72
Google	71
Adobe	46
Vonage	45
Verizon Wireless	40
Charles Schwab	36
AT&T	11

Apple has 83 percent promoters minus 6 percent detractors for a phenomenally high NPS of 77 – number two of all U.S. companies.* Why change a winning formula? What does the pull era and the performance economy mean to Apple? If I start with the company at the top, perhaps that will give you an idea that other companies may need a bit of work as well.

The Computerless Computer Company

Apple has built an "insanely great" twentieth-century company based solidly on the push model. Yet the Apple brand belongs to its customers. If Apple started falling behind their demands, its customers would try to help get it back in front again. And that's good, because the company has gotten so used to making money the old-fashioned way, it can't see the pull train coming. Selling beautiful hardware with songs and operating systems has given Apple tremendous momentum: these cash cows are sure to provide plenty of milk for the next several years. But the company must closely watch the rise in popularity of netbooks and the web-based operating system, because as that curve trends up, their curve will start to trend down.†

It doesn't take a computer scientist to see that there won't be any more Apple or Windows operating systems, at least for end users. These dinosaurs will go extinct as the world of real-time access and streaming to cheap, or even free, displays takes their place. I expect it will be a ten-year process. Soon (but not too soon), Apple will need to stop

---

*Unless you're in the military, you won't guess what number one is.

†IBM figured out long ago that services will be more profitable than hardware, and they continue to push the adoption of semantic web technologies: Visit **IBM.com/think** to see how they have already built a computerless computer company and are already entering the performance economy.

designing state-of-the-art hardware and start designing insanely great data centers. We the customers don't need laptops with ever-bigger hard disks and expensive phones with more storage. We won't want to pay to make a phone call to anywhere. We're going to need access to everything, native on the web, in real time, all the time. And the applications will run on the server, not on the handset.

Apple's biggest asset is not the Mac or the iPhone but the overall Apple experience. The Apple experience is excellent, but it is still a fairly solitary one – it's far from the collaborative platform it will need to be. It doesn't pass our semantic acid test, because many of the programs people use have proprietary formats and treat the computer as a stand-alone machine. To Apple, the iPhone is another proprietary platform with hardware vendor lock-in at the center of the strategy. As I write this, you can't even add more memory to an i-Phone.

Nor should you want to. You don't need much memory for storage if your data store is the entire web. The proprietary approach has served Apple well for more than twenty-five years, but it will soon become a liability as people start using ultra-cheap machines to do everything online.

Apple's next big chance is in publishing. At the moment, publishing software runs on workstations that are connected to the web, but the entire platform is just a virtual version of the way documents were designed and produced in the days of Stanley Morison, the designer of Times Roman. The pull approach will be highly collaborative and much more productive. It will use open formats that don't yet exist to define the *kind* of document you are making before you add the content. As the music industry is just starting to learn, creatives will have to find new methods of design and expression for the pull era – the push approach won't work. Whatever is left of publishing in the future will take place in a collaborative workspace online, dedicated to the specific task at hand, where the document or product stays put and all the services and content flow in as needed. If Apple were to build this platform and open the standards, it would be well on the way to staying relevant for the next twenty-five years.

You've probably guessed my most important recommendation. Apple should replace all its consumer-professional hardware and operating systems with an online Macintosh data locker and semantic dashboard that its customers will trust with their financial, health, career, education, professional, and personal data. It's not a matter of web design and focusing on services. It requires the birth certificates, standards, and open tools I've described elsewhere in this book. The accounts will have to be portable, and the company should be on the side of the customer at all times. Apple may continue to make hardware and sell it below cost (as it does with the iPhone), and make up the difference with a lock-in contract for services. But eventually, when we're really in the performance economy, the hardware will be far too cheap for Apple to stay in that game. In the long run, Apple will be better off as a computerless computer company.

Performance Account Management

In the performance economy:

It will be as easy to downgrade your account as to upgrade.

It will be easy to take your entire account to a competitor.

Customers will be notified of recurring charges several days ahead of time, with the easy option to opt out or downgrade before they occur.

A customer's bill of rights will be made explicit.

Customers will have a voice on the policies of the company.

Companies will establish a customer council to represent customers in all high-level discussions.

If Apple is willing to embrace that much change, it should hang onto its "insanely great" Net Promoter Score. The biggest change will be cultural – the company must adopt a more open approach to working with partners and customers than ever before. It must be willing to kiss its proprietary sacred cows good-bye as the milk dries up. And the only charismatic leader it will need is one who will listen to the customers and let them lead the way.

Performance Money

What if I told you that I had invented a new kind of credit card: it has a high interest rate, it has your name on the front, and on the back – printed in large letters – is the PIN code you need to validate it and charge something. Does that sound good to you? That's exactly what we have today in the United States – your credit card has your name on the front, and on the back, believe it or not, is your signature, showing anyone who gets your credit card how to forge your signature to make a purchase.*

Although credit card companies claim to be on our side, they simply charge higher fees to reclaim the money they lose through fraud. Americans pay an average 14 percent APR on credit cards[38] and more than $18 billion per year in credit-card penalty fees.[39] Credit card companies routinely sell portfolios of consumer debt to help hedge their businesses.

In the pull era, the power distribution shifts toward the consumer.

---

* Studies find fraud rates are four to fifteen times higher for signature-based cards than for PIN-based cards. PIN-based transactions generally settle on the same day, while signature-based transactions can take a week or more. According to a Unisys study, the United States leads the world in identity fraud, with 17 percent of consumers saying they have been victims.

One company, **Revolution Money**, aims to fill the gap. Backed by Steve Case and $50 million in venture capital, the company offers its RevolutionCard with more security features, no annual fee, and a reasonable annual percentage rate, depending on your credit score. My RevolutionCard is silver. It has no name or signature, only an account number printed on the front and encoded into the magnetic stripe on the back. I need a PIN to activate it, and it's already accepted by hundreds of thousands of merchants. If I lose it, it's impossible to trace or use without the PIN. While credit card companies normally charge the merchant between 2 and 3.5 percent and often include a per-transaction fee, RevolutionMoney only charges the merchant 0.5 percent.

Using Revolution MoneyExchange, I can transfer money to anyone who also has an account. It's free to get an account, and free to transfer money between your checking account and your RME account. If it can gain enough exposure, Revolution Money could give PayPal and Western Union a run for their money.

Like other forms of payment, my RevolutionCard will eventually be a virtual i-card that enables e-cash and e-coin payments in small amounts. If I want to buy something online, leave a tip for a blogger, or read a newsletter for a dollar, I'll apply my Revolution i-card in just a few seconds – the PIN is already securely in the i-card, making quick transactions possible. Eventually, I'll leave my physical card at home and pay from my mobile phone using my Revolution i-card, credit card, or any other method I choose.

If it takes off, Revolution Money Exchange has most of the hallmarks I'm looking for in a first-generation pull payment system, except that it's not built on open standards and your account isn't portable. You can hardly blame the company. Eventually, I hope, RME's platform will widen as it gets traction, so we can build secure transaction and payment options on open standards for use around the world. (Get yours at **RevolutionCard.com.**)

Two Key Questions

Remember the dinner-ordering scenario? Look at it from a supplier's viewpoint. Your customer is going to say, "We want something new today," or "Surprise me," or "Looking for the best price on some semantically specified product or service delivered Thursday," or "We decided to add another floor to the building plan," or "That didn't work – help!" That's what an order is going to look like. I hope you can see how underprepared you are for those requests.

And that's okay. We're all unprepared, but now is the time to start preparing. So to get going, let's ask two questions that will flip us from push to pull and from today's inefficient economy to the performance economy of tomorrow:

Question 1: Is your company willing to embrace true account portability?

This is something you can start on today. Account portability is the twenty-first-century approach to marketing; don't wait to be dragged into it.

Question 2: Are you willing to make money if you help your customers and make less or no money if you don't help them?

My guess is that you'll say you'd love to do business that way, but it doesn't work. That's a reasonable response. But there will be a way. Your customers are happy to pay a premium for results. If you learn to deliver them before your competitors do, you'll stay in the game and keep your customers. If someone else figures it out, you'll learn how loyal your customers really are. Just getting past the denial phase and into learning mode is a good start.

While the principles of pull will help companies use information every day, the performance economy is a general mind-set that always looks for win-win situations rather than making actuarial calculations. If your answer is yes to those two questions, you're going to do very well in the performance economy.

The Performance Labor Market

Not long ago, I went to pick up my x-ray results from Dr. A so I could take them and show them to Dr. B. I called Dr. A's office, and a guy named Kenny said I could come pick up the DVD with my x-rays on it. I said, "That's how it's done these days? I walk into my new doctor's office carrying a DVD?" Kenny said, "Yes, that's how you do it."

I said, "I guess eventually, the image data will automatically go to a server, and I'll access it any time I want. That's progress, isn't it?"

Kenny replied, "When that day comes, I'll be out of a job."

I'm confident he'll find a good one. People all over the country who are used to physically handling, changing, or maintaining metadata will have to find other ways to contribute to our national output. The quartz watch movement challenged the Swiss to overhaul their concept of what a watch is and what role it plays in the consumer's life. Their response – the Swatch – catapulted them back into a leadership position. The first Internet wave eliminated many jobs and probably created even more. As the semantic web firms up, intelligent agents will do more and more of our administrative and clerical work, replacing an entire class of human labor, reshaping our economy in ways even I can't predict. It will take more than ten years, but eventually our software will do all the mechanical drudgework for us, making a single knowledge worker perhaps hundreds of times more productive than she is today.

Where will the jobs go? I have identified at least $2 trillion worth of waste in our civilian economy, which accounts for at least 50 million jobs in the United States alone. Europe will have a proportionate displacement. What will people do? Is it really progress, or will it lead to mass unemployment and a worldwide recession?

I don't think we have too much to worry about. Even though the power shift will be disruptive to many industries, the overall effect will be gradual, and plenty of new jobs will open as a result. Just as the computer revolution took a good thirty years to bring us the tools we have today, the semantic web will take that long to reshape our economy.

If we can pass the FairTax, a lot of well-educated accountants will have to find jobs. Just as Swiss firms had to embrace the quartz watch to regain dominance in their industry, accountants will quickly find new ways to add value to our economy. The FairTax alone will help companies rebuild here in the United States, creating many high-paying manufacturing and service-sector jobs. And it will repatriate more than $10 trillion of wealth, which will certainly create more jobs here than if it stayed offshore. We could easily end up with more jobs than we lose.

In the performance economy, people like Kenny will do the real work of tagging, categorizing, and cleansing data, rather than distributing it. *That's* progress, and it will give people around the world a chance to participate in a globally connected, interdependent economy.

What's Next?

The car of the future will run on two things: electricity and information. It may make its electricity on board by burning fuel, or it will get it from the grid. But the information component is where we'll find the real improvements. Your car's "brain" will live in your online data locker, so any car is your car – it has your transport ontology on board at all times. It knows where you've been, how many tickets you have, and what the traffic and weather are like, and it knows not only where you are going but also what you're trying to accomplish. It gets smarter every time you drive, even if you're driving someone else's car. We'll use satellites to charge for parking rather than the coin-based meters we use today. Once customers start using their data lockers, they'll start demanding more performance from everything they own.

In April 2009, a swine flu virus spread quickly from Mexico City to dozens of countries. Within *three business days*, there was a tradable stock index that let you buy a basket of swine flu–related stocks in a single trade. This is not your grandmother's metadata! We can't get ahead of these trends by doing what we did before, only faster. In the performance economy, everything will assemble and disassemble from small, reusable modules to meet unpredictable demands in real time.

17: One Big Step

Pull Concept: Start with Small Steps

> *When I was an undergraduate at MIT we shared one computer that took up a whole building. The cell phone in your pocket is a million times cheaper and a thousand times more powerful. That's a billion times the sales performance – and we'll do it again in the next 25 years.**
>
> *– Ray Kurzweil*

IN THE EARLY 1990S, I made a good living from font royalties. By the middle of the decade, the market was dead. Plenty of people still want and use fonts, but no one pays for them anymore. Total revenues for the worldwide market are so low that people like me, who had spent ten years learning the craft, had to go design web sites and annual reports. Fortunately for me, the implosion of the font market put me ahead of the curve in the online revolution, and I was able to take advantage of it. In the words of ex-governor Richard Lamm of Colorado, "There are boat problems and river problems. You can't solve a river problem by fixing your boat."

Almost no one is immune to this effect. It will take time, but these

---

* One billion times one billion in one lifetime – that's 1,000 quadrillion, or 1 quintillion.

changes are aiming to flatten your industry. It could happen to you sooner than later. Books, music, real-estate, advertising, catalogs, manufacturing, computers, software, supply chains, and probably your industry are about to change so completely that we won't recognize them in ten years.

The tsunami is coming. After reading this book, I hope you're convinced that we all need to do something about it. Many jobs will be lost, and many will be created. We need to start now, taking small steps toward an uncertain goal. We need to find the middle path, between becoming semantic zealots throwing the baby out with the bathwater and becoming deer in the headlights, frozen in place, not knowing what to do. My goal in this chapter is for you to take the first step toward change. If it feels risky, you're doing something right. If someone wants to sell you the latest "semantic-web technology," your semantic bullshit detector should be able to tell whether he's taking you in the right direction.

Business Strategy First, Technology Second

Managers will say, "Why should I put this year's budget into making improvements that won't show up for a few years?" We'll need to take a long-term approach to the semantic web and gear up appropriately. That's why I hope upper-level managers will make this book their secret weapon: these projects work much better with support from the top. Just as we invested in web technology in the mid-1990s, we will need another round of investment to cross the chasm from push to pull. Every company has work to do. Several well-known brands won't survive because management wasn't forward-looking enough. To review, the main principles of pull are:

Organize around customers and customer groups, not capabilities.

Fit into your customers' environment. Let your customers contribute to your metadata and pull it into their systems.

Never duplicate information. Each person and organization puts its own information on the open web in a standard format sharing a common name space.

Pay for performance and results rather than process.

Automatically generate metadata in a sharable, reusable format as you go about your business, including transactions.

Ask questions and get answers, rather than search for keywords, products, web sites.

Apply the semantic web acid test:

> Is it semantic (*using an unambiguous, tagged, open-data format*)?

> Is it on the web, *as opposed to in a database*?

Start now. Put your core team together with a few early adopters at all levels in the organization. Better to get a small group committed to producing results and widen the project as it becomes more visible. To find the right people, look beyond your company. Look for semantic web business groups forming online, and start one yourself if you don't find one that works for you. Look for co-conspirators online. Look for others in your industry who will become champions of industry realignment. Better to work with a sharp person at one of your competitors than to try to convince your colleagues who aren't ready yet.

Starter Projects

Because each industry is going at its own pace, I can't give you a definitive transition time line. The next phase in planning your semantic road map is to get started on some projects that will be a platform for further development. Plan for the next two years, and break it into manageable pieces with short time horizons.

Repeat after me: It's not about technology. It's about changing from fossilized processes to goal-driven, customer-centered management objectives. Doing nothing is more dangerous in the long run. Here are some possible steps to get the ball rolling.

Conduct a semantic boot camp for the forward thinkers in your company. Two days of learning and one day of translating the concepts into a road map for your company will help get your advance team going.

Measure the gap and close it. Close the gap between what happens to the metadata and what happens in the real world. It should take less than a minute from when something (anything) changes to when you see it on your dashboard. Your ultimate goal should be real time. (For starters, visit YAMMER.COM.)

Scrub your data. Go to a data governance conference. Join the validation process for common data standards. Bring in consultants to find inaccuracies and insist on a Six Sigma approach to data integrity. Measure your data integrity in errors per million and keep reducing that number.

Support data portability in your industry. The first step toward open standards is data portability. Eventually, the semantic web will require a complete overhaul of your IT infrastructure. Don't tell your IT people that! Just tell them data portability is the next big thing and that your company needs to participate.

Initiate account portability. If you look for signs of account portability in your industry, you'll find them. At the very least, you should keep this topic on your radar and discuss it from time to time. Get serious about it now and reap the rewards sooner than others in your company think.

Make your company and its products and services more findable. Start by establishing a single location for each description of every product or service, and don't change the name of that location. Make sure other software can count on its being there. Audit your web site for findability and semantic standards.

Identify your proprietary standards and start to eliminate them. Join the consortium in your business areas and commit to common data standards, inside and outside of your company. These standards should eventually be native, not imported, to your system.

Stop throwing good money after bad. Stop reprogramming your systems every time there's a new business requirement. Start an adaptive approach that weans you off the hardwired programming that's been costing so much money.

Join as many competitors as you can in a pilot project. It's better to take small steps as a group than it is to try to get ahead of everyone else.

Build a business vocabulary, or adopt one. There are plenty to choose from. There are low-level vocabularies and taxonomies being built right now. Go with whatever has the most momentum and help make it better. Help fight semantic dispersion.

Build web-scale services. Become part of the semantic ecosystem by providing what you do well to others, using open shared standards. Put some of your core assets online as a service and give them away to anyone who wants them. See where it takes you.

Build some bad software that does things semantically and improve it later. Spreadsheets are low-hanging fruit. Wherever you find a spreadsheet doing production work, you've discovered a process that's been broken for some time.

Help build the ROI for semantic projects. Share information with others in your industry. Write up what you have learned. The more we can share, the better.

Build a road map to the semantic web. You have most of what you need right here in this book. You may not know what the dates are, but much of what I've talked about should give an initial compass heading for where you need to go. You don't need all the details, but you can still write down your intentions. As an example, the city of Vancouver has done it on their own, and the story is worth telling.

The Open City

In May 2009, the city of Vancouver passed a nonbinding motion that immediately gave it the most open and progressive public-data agenda of any city in the world. The full text of the motion reads like a summary of Part II of this book:

> Be it resolved that the City of Vancouver endorses the principles of:
>
> **Open and accessible data:** The City of Vancouver will freely share with citizens, businesses, and other jurisdictions the greatest amount of data possible while respecting privacy and security concerns.
>
> **Open standards:** The City of Vancouver will move as quickly as possible to adopt prevailing open standards for data, documents, maps, and other formats of media.
>
> **Open-source software:** The City of Vancouver, when replacing existing software or considering new applications, will place open-source software on an equal footing with commercial systems during procurement cycles.
>
> Be it further resolved that in pursuit of open data the City of Vancouver will:
>
> Identify immediate opportunities to distribute more of its data.
>
> Index, publish, and syndicate its data to the Internet using prevailing open standards, interfaces, and formats.

Develop a plan to digitize and freely distribute suitable archival data to the public.

Ensure that data supplied to the City by third parties (developers, contractors, consultants) are unlicensed, in a prevailing open standard format, and not copyrighted except if otherwise prevented by legal considerations.

License any software applications developed by the City of Vancouver such that they may be used by other municipalities, businesses, and the public without restriction.

Vancouver now has a road map to better data integration and the semantic web. City and supporting services will change as a result. Vancouver will influence other governments and spread the word. It may not use the words "pull" or "semantic web," but this city is on the track to the performance economy.

The Bottom Billion

More and more, people in the developing world are getting access to computers and buying mobile phones. In the pull future, people will improve their circumstances using cheap displays and Internet access. *If we send anything to Africa, it should be Internet access.* Once the people of Africa have bandwidth, they will be able to take advantage of the web of data we're building now. Here are just a few examples.

Education. Basic educational materials are not affordable in many places. Imagine what will happen to Uganda when Kampala gets the first machine that can print any book ever written for just a few dollars. Imagine what will happen when kids can take their $10 screens home (one screen per child) and see the entire Internet for the price of cranking the handle.

Transferring money. According to the World Bank, remittances from U.S. citizens to developing countries are over $160 billion. I estimate the transfer fees on that to be in the neighborhood of $15 billion (Western Union captures $5 billion per year alone). In the semantic future, we'll move money between data lockers using our mobile phones, eliminating the need for companies like Western Union.

Health care. In Rwanda, the Clinton Foundation and others have put together a partnership to improve rural health care. One of the cornerstones of the project is a system of health records for each patient. Using open standards for patient records and servers hosted in the United States, the system operates easily from any browser – all you need is a PC and an Internet connection.

Setting up a commodities or stock market. In markets for cash crops, information is more valuable than the crops themselves. In many markets, the middlemen end up taking most of the profits, while the farmers have slim or unsustainable margins. In the pull era, you can set up a commodities market in a day and use mobile phones to get prices. Everything you need will already be online.

Microfinance. Today, web sites like Kivu, Prosper, and Microplace help loan money to small businesses. Each site has its own terms and reputation system to rate lenders and borrowers. By putting loans on a web-wide footing, we will make more needs and more lenders discoverable.

Ad-Hoc infrastructure. According to Stewart Brand in his book, *Whole Earth Discipline*, 1.3 million people are flowing into the world's cities every *week*. By 2050, a billion people will be living in squatter cities. As they come to the cities seeking opportunity, they pick up mobile phones. They start to exchange information. The principles of this book will let this part of the infosphere expand to meet new demands dynamically as they are created. Spontaneously, mesh networks will arise around new standards and tie into each other without much planning. By the middle of this century, your personal ontology could not only *reflect* where you live, how much you make, who your friends are, and what options you have, it could also *determine* them.

Voting. I predict that a nonprofit will build a scalable voting system that can be used worldwide. The scenario: Every person in every country gets a free voting i-name. Once the provisioning is done, either by governments or NGOs, your ID and password would be all you need to vote. The voting system itself would be secure and couldn't be tampered with because it would be maintained in a neutral location by the voting organization, which would tally results and send them back. People could just vote on their phones, the way Estonians do now. In the era of pull, the best voting machine is – you guessed it – no voting machine at all.

Tagging. The world's metadata will need a lot of tagging. Anyone with a mobile phone and a little training can improve metadata all day, even from a wheelchair or a goat pasture, and get paid for it.

Government transparency. As more information goes onto the open web, it will be harder for governments to shield illegal transfers. Donors will insist that money and information be more trackable, transactions more transparent. The principles of pull will help make that a reality.

To give you food for thought in constructing your road map, I now present my closing arguments: four high-level concepts I hope will keep you on track as you make the power shift from push to pull.

Lose the Silo Mentality

The CTO says: "Just tell me what the new requirements are, and I'll build tools to support it." But that's more of a silo mentality; it's not how the pull model works. In the pull model, the tools don't change that much, even though the requirements change all the time. The tools are adaptive. They are an entirely new *breed* of tool. They start to change the moment you use them. The processes change constantly. Every time you go through a process, you make it different and better for the next person, even if that person is your competitor.

We can expand the concept of data silos (databases, web sites) to the rest of our lives. **Silos** are independent functional units that have their own support structures. They're not just for storing information. They're for compartmentalizing learning, work, play, religion, government, business, even thought and knowledge. They influence our approach to problem solving more than they should. Here are examples of silos in action:

States

The school of engineering

Marketing

The IRS

The army

FEDEX

The legal department

Your doctor's office

AutoCad

Web sites

Databases

Brands

Silos are everywhere, yet they rarely solve problems by themselves. People have real problems; they need real solutions. They don't want to cobble solutions together manually most of the time. We should replace silos with systems – systems that can learn and evolve and draw from many different resources to solve problems. Schools, for example, could be oriented around real-life issues, like water, environment, cities, food, information, money, transportation, entertainment, governance, etc. I have always thought that school curricula should be oriented around projects and simulations, not tests, because there are no tests in the real world. How can we raise the next generation of competitive innovators when we are building a nation of young people who are skilled at choosing the correct answer among the four given?

Wherever you find tests, you find the old push mentality. The world is now moving too fast for tests. People assemble around problems, come together, get something done with people contributing many different skills, then they break up and go form other ad hoc problem-solving teams. In the school of the future, I hope students will build bridges, go to Mars, respond to emergencies, renovate office buildings, dive to the bottom of the ocean, plan an Olympic Games, propose alternatives to the president of Rwanda in 1986 to try to avoid genocide, and other historical, fictional, and current projects that will teach them what it takes to get results in the real world. In this project-based learning environment, students will learn new skills quickly because they must. They will learn to lead at times and follow at others. Silo learning is no longer relevant. Adaptability and tenacity are often more important than specific expertise.

It's time to blow up the silos. It's time to build in flexibility. It's time to get our economy running. Look for silos in your organization and your life – they are a measure of how much work we have left to do.

Build in Autonomy

You've probably noticed a basic principle emerging from the trends in this book: a movement from hierarchical or central control structures to increased autonomy. Whether it's your own personal music ontology, robotic ants, buildings doing their own inspections, packages flowing through the shipstream, or corporate teams with the goal of accomplishing objectives rather than following procedure, more people and things will become autonomous. It's not through the virtues of futuristic artificial intelligence – it's that our data lockers and devices have the information available and can make sense of it thanks to the semantic web.

According to the National Air Traffic Controllers Association, about 15,000 controllers assure the safe takeoff and landing of some 90,000 flights per day over the United States. While air traffic is expected to double by 2020, the number of controllers will stay the same, or potentially even go down.

How is that possible? The current radar-based control system, set up in the 1930s, puts pilots at the center, but with tremendous constraints. When a pilot wants to change course or altitude, she uses the radio to get permission from the controller, who makes sure two planes don't get too close to each other. Because a plane can move a mile in any direction between radar passes, minimum spacing of aircraft is three miles, and the airspace "highways" and "on-off ramps" are designed for three-mile spacing. This voice-driven system is already past its breaking point.

Over the next fifteen years, the FAA will switch to a suite of independent, satellite-based, data-driven technologies, collectively called **NextGen**. The system will show all neighboring aircraft in a cockpit display, giving the pilot more information with many fewer radio calls. The GPS-based system will reduce spacing from three miles to one mile and allow pilots to take more control of the landing process.

UPS now has more than 100 planes using NextGen equipment, and most of them arrive in Louisville after dark. In the old voice-driven system, pilots had to follow a step-down program on approach, waiting for the signal from the controller, flying at low altitudes and wasting fuel while arriving at irregular intervals from 90 to 180 seconds.

UPS pilots now see all the terrain, weather, and planes on a single screen. They have primary responsibility for spacing and use "continuous descent" procedures that save fuel. By working together, pilots now land their planes in consistent 95-second intervals. The company expects to save over 800,000 gallons of fuel annually, reduce noise by 30 percent, and cut its emissions by 34 percent below 3,000 feet, increasing the capacity of the Louisville airport by 15 percent or more. United Airlines and other carriers are already equipping flights for autonomous guidance over water, where there are no ground stations.

If you've been on a commercial flight encountering turbulence, you may have heard the captain announce it in advance. This "information" is based on anecdotal reporting to ground controllers that is fed back by voice. Using NextGen, the planes themselves contribute to a "turbulence map" of real-time data, letting pilots make many small real-time adjustments rather than sudden big adjustments based on information coming in too late. As the FAA has recognized, people will come up with ways to use the system they haven't thought of yet, and they are designing the data architecture to support that. NextGen will increase efficiency while keeping travel safe and can scale up to meet the needs of the twenty-first century.

The trend is clear – we're going from centralized control of metadata to autonomy and independence. We're going to see mesh networks and data maps spring up to meet new demands. Many industries consolidate because of the so-called scale efficiencies of combining the back offices, but that's because ERP software is so heavy and hard to manage. In the world of pull, every company, from the largest to a single sole proprietor, uses the same software and the same cloud-based data, without the expense of IT departments keeping everything working.

Public-Private Partnerships

In March 1902, a court invalidated Thomas Edison's claim to a patent on the 35-millimeter film format he had invented.[40] Edison wasn't pleased, but it was the right business decision. The format had already become a de facto standard for still and motion pictures, essentially providing a solid link between cameras and film-processing equipment, and between movie cameras and projectors. Free from having to pay royalties, engineers began innovating on the design of still cameras, movie cameras, and projectors around a common format.*

In the end, Edison did just fine, and the width of a strip of film became a public asset. In researching this book, I was disappointed to learn how much the states enjoy their autonomy, preventing federal standards that could make the country far more productive. We can learn a lot from Europe. The North American and Asian countries should join them in building more international standards.†

In the aftermath of the economic meltdown of 2008 and the recession of 2009, business and government are going to be partners more than ever before. As the world globalizes, our standards bodies and governments need much more support to help make the switch from push to pull. We should take a longer, more collaborative view of the value of information to the human enterprise. If I have one wish, it's that a group like the Clinton Foundation or George Soros's Open Society Institute or the Electronic Frontier Foundation will put together a platform for bringing people from many countries and many industries together in the spirit of cooperation to build the public-private partnerships that will accelerate the building of a global infrastructure for semantic data. We need public resources like Mark Bolgiano's US GAAP taxonomy in *every* field. The energy and tools will come from the private sector, but nonprofit stewardship of data standards will become the cornerstone of the world I describe in this book.

These standards will become national and global assets upon which much of our twenty-first-century economy will be based. I believe the future of the banking system, health care, transportation, trade, and

---

*There are actually more than a hundred different film formats, but we're lucky we don't live in a world where each manufacturer sells its own special film with its cameras.

†As of 2008, all countries in the world have officially adopted the metric system for measurement, save three: the United States, Burma, and Liberia.

many other fields will need a solid foundation on which to build. We should heed the warnings we've been given and start to take these collective assets more seriously.

One Big Step

The next step is not a small evolutionary one, yet it's not a nuclear-powered explosion of semantic activity either. We have a few trillion dollars of inefficiency to take out of our economy, but if we can learn to type using the Dvorak keyboard layout, we can learn to do anything. It took ten years and more than 400,000 people for the United States to put a man on the moon, but we did it. You could say it took many small steps, then one big step, then many more small steps.*

The big step in bowling took place in the 1980s. The big step in books happened around 2000. Several retailers already require RFIDs at the pallet level. The big step for financial reporting happened in 2009. In many areas of research, we're just a few years away. Passive commerce and mass customization are still five to ten years out. Microformats are popular for résumés, and there are already hundreds of millions of OpenIDs in use. Governments are leading the way with research and standards efforts. Central repositories and linked data are already supporting several industries. The FairTax is gaining supporters. Companies and agencies are experimenting with i-names and i-cards.

---

*The big step was the first manned orbital flight by Yuri Gagarin, on April 12, 1961, which prompted an irresolute President John F. Kennedy to declare six weeks later the U.S. goal of landing a man on the moon by the end of the decade. Many small steps later, astronaut Neil Armstrong made a giant leap for mankind on July 21, 1969.

At some point, we'll look back and realize it's generally happened – we're pushing less and pulling more. We are starting to talk about performance and outcomes. We're starting to talk about agility on a new scale. We're starting to talk about *everything* on a new scale. Then, it's just a series of small steps until much of what I have envisioned here is part of everyday life.

Many small steps.

Then one big step.

Then many more small steps.

In our lives and in the world, everything is connected to everything. In our data and in the online world, we are about to catch up to that reality. Using information wisely, we have a chance to use resources more efficiently and be kinder to the planet as the population peaks toward the end of this century. Come take the next step for your company.

ThePowerofPull.com
David@ThePowerofPull.com
=siegel

Acknowledgments

THIS BOOK WAS A TWO-YEAR JOURNEY. Almost every major business publisher had a chance to bring this book to market and turned it down. I am deeply grateful to Adrian Zackheim for his support of my vision and my ability to connect with readers. His capable team, including my faithful editor Courtney Young, believed in this project from the day they read the first terrible draft. They gave me the room to develop and design the book the way I wanted it.

Thomas Davenport brought me to the attention of Hollis Heimbouch, who saw the vision and loved it. Even though we didn't end up as partners, her support helped me write the early drafts that brought the project to Adrian's attention. Tim O'Reilly helped by turning down the project but then friending me on Facebook and pointing me to several fascinating developments.

Hundreds of people contributed to this book. Many contributed to chapters that didn't make the cut. My faithful researcher, David Wineberg, chased everything down and argued relentlessly for me to make the book more relevant to business people. My brother Rob read it many times and contributed to the health-care chapter. My many test readers suffered through jargon-filled drafts, hoping I would simplify. All the people I interviewed were gracious with their time and helped me paint this picture of a world that doesn't yet exist. Mills Davis of Project10x was particularly helpful in redlining early drafts. Jason Chan contributed throughout as usual. Brian Wu hung in there through dozens of cover designs. Kaliya and Drummond spent weeks explaining layers of Internet security. Many members of the semantic web movement, from Esther Dyson to Nova Spivack, encouraged me to go the distance and get the message out. Charlie Hoffman, David vun Kannon, and Mark Bolgiano spent endless hours with me explaining XBRL. Mark Lesswing at the National Association of Realtors helped keep me honest. Frances Haugen at Google and all the people in the book industry were very generous with their time. Amy Gorin and Hugh Wallis helped make it more accurate. All my friends on Facebook cheered me on as the word count mounted, then shrunk back.

Finally, my wife, Beatrice, whom I married and had a child with during the course of writing this book, is the true hero of the project. She supported me fully during the days, nights, and months of writing. When she had a hungry child and a thousand things to do, she let me put on my headset and interview yet another person around the world by Skype, giving me the time I needed to put everything in place.

Notes

The links to the articles, shown in bold type, were up to date as this book went into production. Just type them into your browser window as they appear here. However, you'll find all the links and any corrections at **ThePowerofPull.com** – so come to the web site and click, rather than typing in the URLs here.

1. From Michael Bergman's highly recommended paper *Untapped Assets: The $3 Trillion Value of U.S. Documents*, July 2005. See: http://www.brightplanet.com/pdf/Docu mentsValue.pdf.
2. Source: Bowl.com. With the possible exception of soccer, bowling is the most popular participatory sport in the world and has far more registered competitors than any other sport. In the United States, it is a $10 billion industry.
3. As of 2004, over 200 million computers are sold in the United States every year; see http://arstechnica.com/articles/culture/total-share.ars.
4. See "Chris's Dvorak Keymap Rant" at http://homepages.ihug.co.nz/~jedwards /Chris/Dvorak.html; see also "The Dvorak Simplified Keyboard: Forty Years of Frustration," by Robert Parkinson, in *Computers and Automation* magazine, November 1972 (http://infohost.nmt.edu/~shipman/ergo/parkinson.html).
5. I have been typing Dvorak for fifteen years. I type at least twice as fast with Dvorak as with QWERTY, and with fewer aches and pains. To change to Dvorak, start here: http://www.wikihow.com/Switch-to-a-Dvorak-Keyboard-Layout.
6. This figure came from a conversation with the salesperson who worked for UPS at the time.
7. Dell Annual Report.
8. According to FEDEX's 2007 annual report, that company spent $445 million on vehicles. In an interview with EyeForTransport.com, Tim Geiken, VP of e-commerce for

UPS, said, "The company spends over $1 billion a year on information technology – more than we spend on trucks."

9. Source: conversation with a UPS consultant and online documents that are no longer available.

10. Learn more about UPC and its RFID counterpart, the EPC, at http://gs1.org.

11. Figures from this chapter on GDSN come from www.1synch.org – the GS1 hub for information on GDSN.

12. See http://www.bridge-project.eu/.

13. See http://tryxbrl.com.

14. See http://www.quantcast.com. In spring 2009, Goodreads had by far the highest traffic figures, with 1.2 million visits and over 21 million page views monthly.

15. OCLC 2007–2008 annual report, which is available at http://www.oclc.org/news/publications/annualreports/.

16. According to WorldWideWebSize.com, Google indexes about 16 billion web pages.

17. The figures on public, deep, and private webs all come from a single 2000 Berkeley study and are shamefully out of date. Google and Yahoo won't publish figures. The original figures are 1 billion, 400 billion, and 200 billion pages, respectively. Researchers seem content with these ancient figures, which are at this point meaningless. I have multiplied all the numbers by 16 to give an approximation of where we are today and to show the magnitude of the differences. No one has any idea how big the deep or private webs are, much less how much information is on a "page."

18. Tom Vanderbilt, "Datatecture," *The New York Times Magazine,* June 14, 2009.

19. You can find this statistic in many places. It's included in a great report on Internet privacy done by the Online Computer Library Center, a resource on web-related issues for librarians. Its free 2007 report, *Sharing, Privacy, and Trust in Our Networked World,* is a very interesting read and is available at www.OCLC.org.

20. *Undeliverable-As-Addressed (UAA) Mail Cost Study-Executive Summary:* http://ribbs.usps.gov/files/UAA/UAASUM.pdf.

21. KPMG Analysis: Kathleen Kiley, "Retailers Find That Customized Clothing Is the Right Fit," *Consumer Markets Insider,* 2006. (Article no longer available.)

22. This is just a press release, but it seems there's enough commercial interest to take the next step: http://www.medlaunches.com/gadgets/scientist_create_computer_pill.php. I'd love to say that in the pull paradigm the best pillow is – no pillow at all! But that would be silly and result in too many sore necks.

23. I strongly encourage readers to read Michael Bergman's blogs and white papers at MKBergman.com. This statistic on search comes from *Why are $800 Billion in Document Assets Wasted Annually?* See: http://www.brightplanet.com/images/stories/pdf/wasteddocumentassets.pdf.

24. From the Compete blog: http://blog.compete.com/2007/09/26/search-queries-results-yahoo-google-msn-live/.

25. See: http://www.google.com/jobs/britney.html.

26. Source: Kelsey Group report available by subscription; for a summary see techcrunch

.com/2008/02/26/estimates-put-internet-advertising-at-21-billion-in-US-45-billion-globally/.

27. Savings of digital signatures: http://www.p2pays.org/ref/17/16437.pdf.

28. Source: "Patients First. Doctors Second," The Health Care Blog, April 30, 2009, http://www.thehealthcareblog.com.

29. See:http://www.washingtonpost.com/wp-dyn/content/article/2009/02/09/AR2009 020903263_2.html.

30. Source: conversations and correspondence with Dr. Deborah Peel, PatientPrivacy Rights.org.

31. My estimate, based on exploring details from various annual reports. Dr. Peel says it is much higher, but all companies hide their data sales, so it's impossible to tell.

32. Source: Nilsonreport.com.

33. See BankRate's 2007 study: http://www.bankrate.com/brm/news/chk/chkstudy/ 20070924_ATM_surcharges_bank_a1.asp.

34. The number of paper checks has fallen from 2004 but is still around 30 billion. See: http://www.fdic.gov/CONSUMERS/CONSUMER/news/cnsum04/cvrstry. html.

35. Jacqueline Duby, Eric Halperin, and Lisa James, "High Cost & Hidden from View: The $10 Billion Overdraft Loan Market," Center for Responsible Lending, May 26, 2005; http://www.responsiblelending.org/overdraft-loans/research-analysis/ip009 -High_Cost_Overdraft-0505.pdf.

36. "Administrative Waste in the U.S. Healthcare System in 2003," by David Himmelstein, Steffie Woolhander, and Sidney Wolfe, in *International Journal of Health Services* 1:34 (2004), http://www.pnhp.org/news/IJHS_State_Paper.pdf.

37. Source: Satmetrix report, March 2009. These reports are available by subscription, without which I could not get the relevant citation. The summary press release (which doesn't have a stable URL) is available by searching satmetrix.com.

38. Source: http://www.indexcreditcards.com/creditcardmonitor/.

39. Revolving credit card debt calculation by Consumer Federation of America, testimony of Travis B. Plunkett before the U.S. Senate, February 2009. Available at consumerfed.org/pdfs/Travis_Plunkett_Testimony_Insurance_Industry_Senate_ Banking_7-29-08.pdf.

40. Wikipedia is probably the best source for this: http://en.Wikipedia.org/wiki/35_ mm_film. The reference there is from: Charles Musser, *The Emergence of Cinema: The American Screen to 1907* (Berkeley: University of California Press, 1994), 303–313.

Index